JOHN PAUL II
SPEAKS TO RELIGIOUS
1993-1994
BOOK VIII

Former Dean of the Faculty of Canon Law at the Gregorian University in Rome and Consultor for various Congregations and Commissions of the Roman Curia, Father Jean Beyer, of the Society of Jesus, is also known for his many works in French on consecrated life and canon law.

This compilation of the texts of John Paul II follows the seven volumes published since 1981, which presented his allocutions to religious during the years 1978-1980 (Book I), 1981-1982 (Book II), 1983-1984 (Book III), 1985-1986 (Book IV), 1987-1988 (Book V), 1989-1990 (Book VI), 1991-1992 (Book VII).

JOHN PAUL II
SPEAKS TO RELIGIOUS
BOOK VIII

PRINCIPAL ALLOCUTIONS AND LETTERS
1993-1994

and

CATECHESES ON
"THE CONSECRATED LIFE"
from the Wednesday General Audiences,
first series: September-December, 1994

Compiled and arranged with a Synopsis

by Father Jean Beyer, S.J.

DISTRIBUTORS

LITTLE SISTERS OF THE POOR

601 Maiden Choice Lane
Baltimore, MD 21228
U.S.A.

2A Meadow Road
South Lambeth
London SW8 1QH
GREAT BRITAIN

Sybil Hill Road
Raheny
Dublin 5
IRELAND

Market Street
P.O. Box 246
Randwick, N.S.W. 2031
AUSTRALIA

INTRODUCTION

This collection originated with the edition of the first ten allocutions of Pope John Paul II to religious.[1] This was a sign of life and a call. The volumes which have been published since then confirm the importance of the religious life in the Church, and the value of giving a deeper instruction on this subject. The homilies, allocutions and letters of the Pope enable a deepening of doctrine which, to an ever greater degree, highlights the essential elements of this life as a consecration to God, and for God, to the salvation of the world.

What appears fundamental to all forms of religious life today is the consecration of one's life by the evangelical counsels, as a total gift, lived in silence and solitude, in the monastic or cloistered life, in fraternal life in community, in apostolic availability, in loving devotedness and assistance to the poor and abandoned of our society.

---

[1] More than 5,000 copies of each of the seven preceding volumes have been distributed. The same collection is published in Spanish and in French.

Even today, the number of religious alone confirms the importance of this call, the value of its witness and the inspiration of this evangelical force in ecclesial life. At present, there are about 800,000 women religious and 200,000 religious men in the Church.

As we have noted, Pope John Paul II always presents the essential elements of religious life with an ever greater emphasis: divine call and free gift, response of love in choosing this life, imitation of Christ, poor, chaste and obedient unto death, on the cross, and the victory assured by the risen Lord, who having ascended to the Father, gives us light and life, peace and joy.

This relationship of love between the Father and the Son is lived in the Spirit of love, the Holy Spirit. This Trinitarian aspect is essential to the consecrated life; it is accentuated by the Pope, who sees religious life in the heart of the Church as a profession of love in the following of Christ. From the beginning of the Church, this has been the nature of the consecrated life. The Pope makes this clear. Did not the apostles abandon all in order to follow Christ and respond to his call? Christ himself, as John Paul II emphasizes, is at the origin of this life completely dedicated to God for the salvation of the world.

The presentation of the catechesis on the consecrated life is an important element of this book. An initial series of talks, given during the Wednesday General Audiences, enables us to deepen our understanding of the nature and evangelical exigencies of this form of life which is lived with an ever increasing awareness in the Church.[2] We hope that the post-synodal exhortation will appear without delay. It will provide a synthesis of the synod as a statement of the Church's doctrine on consecrated life, and will be for religious a new sending forth on mission, a mission in the Church and in the world.

In this Trinitarian perspective expressed by Pope John Paul II, the religious life is revealed, to an ever greater degree, as a loving abandonment to God and, for him, as a gift of charity to others. Rooted in the heart of the Church, this life is essential to its structure. It announces the union with God which will exist in eternity and the communion of love in him. Faithfully lived, the religious life is, already here below, an ardent source of charity, and a light for the world. This is especially true in our time, when only faith expressed through charity attracts and unites those whom God calls to be totally given to the people he saves.

T. Hunger ?. J.

---

[2] Since this catechesis continues into 1995, the remaining talks will be published in the next volume.

INFORMATION CONCERNING
THE SYNOPSIS

The outline and chapter headings (**in Roman numerals**) of the present synopsis are identical to those found in the synopses of the seven preceding books (thus permitting an easier utilization of the series of synopses for a study of the teaching of John Paul II through the years).

Certain topics which appeared in the preceding synopses have not been repeated; others are new*(printed in italics)* and correspond to other aspects of religious and sacerdotal life emphasized by John Paul II during the years 1993 and 1994.

For this reason, the numbering of the topics (**Arabic numerals in bold type appearing at the left hand margin**) does not follow exactly the outline of the preceding synopses.

For each topic, one or several numbers (in regular type) refer the reader to the corresponding paragraphs of the allocutions and letters of the present book.

Information concerning footnotes:
Book I, Book II, etc., refers to the corresponding volumes already published of *"John Paul II Speaks to Religious."*

SYNOPSIS

of the principal allocutions

and letters of

JOHN PAUL II

to religious

and of

the catecheses on the "consecrated life"

1993-1994

Father Jean Beyer, S.J.

ALLOCUTIONS AND LETTERS

1993

CATECHESES FROM
THE GENERAL AUDIENCES ON
"THE CONSECRATED LIFE"

first series: September-December, 1994

PERSONS ADDRESSED
BY JOHN PAUL II

A. To the participants in the Synod on consecrated life, and to the faithful: 166-171; 172-179.

B. To the Conferences of Superiors: 42-48; 101-109.

C. To Religious Institutes:
1. Canons Regular of Prémontré: 33-38.
2. Poor Clare Nuns: 39-41; 66-76.
3. Brothers of Christian Instruction of Ploërmel: 132-135.
4. Capuchin Friars: 94-96; 143-149.
5. Monastic community of Camaldoli: 91-93.
6. Passionists: 159-165.
7. Priests of the Blessed Sacrament: 52-56.
8. Sisters of the Holy Family of Bordeaux: 97-100.

D. To men and women religious: 10-17; 21; 31-32; 110-121.

E. To cloistered religious: 1-9.

F. To priests, religious and seminarians: 26-32; 77-90; 150-158.

G. To priests, religious, seminarians and lay leaders: 18-25.

H. To priests, religious and lay leaders: 49-51.

I. To priests and seminarians: 22-23; 29-30; 57-65.

J. To all the faithful:
122-131; 136-142; General Audiences: 180-187;
188-197; 198-206; 207-213; 214-220; 221-227; 228-235; 236-244; 245-254; 255-262; 263-271.

SYNOPSIS

I— MAGISTERIUM OF JOHN PAUL II

1. Reference to documents of his magisterium:
   a) Redemptor hominis: 160.
   b) Redemptoris missio: 28, 32, 60, 124, 126, 161.
   c) *Veritatis splendor:* 166, 207.
   d) Familiaris consortio: 31, 137, 140, 168, 173.
   e) Redemptionis donum: 31, 163, 200, 217, 230, 234, 239, 242, 247, 255.
   f) Christifideles laici: 168, 173.
   g) Pastores dabo vobis: 29, 58, 59, 60, 61, 63, 102, 129, 168, 173, 210.
   h) Salvifici doloris: 160.
   i) Mulieris Dignitatem: 32, 169.
   j) Potissimum institutioni, Directives on formation in religious Institutes (from the Congregation for Institutes of consecrated life and Societies of apostolic life): 95.
   k) *"Fraternal life in community"* (Congregation for Institutes of consecrated life and Societies of apostolic life, 1994): 263.
   l) Allocutions and messages: 4, 6, 94, 96, 122, 127, 155, 166, 191.
2. Continuity with Paul VI:
   a) Evangelii nuntiandi: 124.
   b) Africae terrarum (1967): 28.
   c) Renovationis causam: 95.
3. Deepening awareness of the Council:
   a) Lumen gentium: 14, 31, 49, 103, 105, 138, 140, 169, 181, 184, 185, 188, 198, 214, 217, 218, 221, 222, 225, 228, 239, 243.
   b) Gaudium et spes: 157.
   c) Presbyterorum Ordinis: 29, 53, 54, 64.
   d) Optatam totius: 30, 63, 138.

II — PARTICULAR CHARISM OF EACH INSTITUTE

III — CHARISM AND ECCLESIAL LIFE

IV — CONSECRATION

V — NATURE OF CONSECRATION THROUGH THE COUNSELS

VI — CONSECRATED LIFE, THEOLOGICAL LIFE

VII — THE EVANGELICAL COUNSELS

VIII — CHRIST AND CONSECRATED LIFE

IX — LIFE IN THE SPIRIT

X — MARY, THE MOTHER AND MODEL OF CONSECRATED LIFE

XI — CONSECRATED LIFE AND APOSTOLATE

XII — ACTION AND CONTEMPLATION

XIII — TYPES OF APOSTOLIC ACTION

XIV — TYPOLOGY OF CONSECRATED LIFE

XV — EREMITICAL LIFE

XVIII — RELIGIOUS PRIESTS

XIX — RELIGIOUS BROTHERS

166. Irreplaceable contribution to the Church: 132, 156.

167. *Authentic consecrated life and professional and ecclesial tasks:* 132, 133.

168. *Community life:* 133.

169. Insertion in the particular Churches: 133.

XX — RELIGIOUS MISSIONARIES

170. Gratitude of the Church toward the missionaries "ad gentes": 27-28, 134.

171. *Missionary zeal, availability to leave one's country:* 148.

XXI — MISSIONARY LIFE

172. Evangelization, mission of the Church which is always relevant: 27-28, 148.

173. *Action of grace for native vocations:* 21, 27, 31.

174. *Importance of monastic life:* 21.

175. Mission of the laity: 19.

176. Ecumenism: 24.

177. *Necessity of a profound spiritual life:* 20.

XXII — RELIGIOUS OF APOSTOLIC LIFE

178. *Feminine apostolic religious life, a gift to the Church:* 43.

179. *Following the first disciples of Christ:* 43, 204-205.

180. Religious and the vocation of the woman: 32, 169.

181. Religious and missionary life: 32, 99.

XXVIII — ECCLESIAL VALUE OF THE RELIGIOUS LIFE

224. *Gift of the Lord to the Church:* 13-14, 88, 109, 144.
225. Charismatic Life: 108, 182-183, 185, 220.
226. Privileged expression of the Church as *Spouse:* 236, 240, 243.
227. Sign and *element* of the holiness of the Church: 14, 21, 39, 167, 178, 185, 187, 207, 220.
228. *Witness of heroic fidelity, even unto martyrdom:* 2, 14-15, 33, 46-47, 88, 118, 153.
229. Necessary witness to the Church and to the world: 39, 41, 116-117, 150-151, 171, 176-177, 188, 207.
230. Variety of religious families, a wealth for the Church: 182.
231. *Approbation by the Church:* 182, 184, 260.
232. Obedience to the Sovereign Pontiff: 261-262.
233. *Filial love and prayer for the Church:* 226, 262.
234. Sign of universality: 108, 148.
235. In the local Church: 51, 108, 133.
236. Contribution to the task of ecumenism: 16, 92, 164.

XXIX — RELIGIOUS LIFE AND SECULAR CLERGY

237. *Favoring communion:* 108, 151.

XXX — RELIGIOUS SUPERIORSHIP

238. *Representatives of God:* 258-260.
239. *Spiritual dispositions required:* 260.
240. Role of the General Chapter: 52, 93, 135, 143.

XXXI — NEW FORMS OF RELIGIOUS LIFE

XXXII — RENEWAL: ITS EXIGENCIES

XXXIII — PRESENT DANGERS AND DIFFICULTIES IN RELIGIOUS LIFE

XXXIV — SECULARIZATION

XXXVIII — FORMATION AND FIDELITY

317. Central place of the Eucharist: 29, 60, 152-153.
318. *Common priesthood and ministerial priesthood:* 180.
319. Necessary service to the Church and to the world: 129, 150-151.

XLII — MISSION OF THE PRIESTHOOD

320. *Participation in the triple mission of Christ:* 65.
321. Guide and master in the faith: 22, 62.
322. *"Pastor of the soul,"* guide of holiness, educator of consciences: 61, 62, 63, 81-83, 85, 87, 156.
323. Man of pardon and reconciliation: 22, 63, 79-80, 152, 154.
324. *Universal mission:* 60.
325. *Ecumenical concern:* 154.
326. Collaboration and formation of the laity: 22, 156.

XLIII — BISHOPS AND PRIESTS

327. Collaborators with the bishop: 22, 29, 50.
328. Priestly fraternity: 50, 64, 151.
329. Communion with the bishop: 50, 65, 151.

XLIV — PRIESTLY SPIRITUALITY

330. Holiness: 83, 151.
331. Union with Christ, life of prayer: 65, 82, 153.
332. Priestly celibacy: 22, 64, 84, 153.
333. Poverty, detachment: 22, 23, 81.
334. *Availability,* sense of the cross: 22, 23, 60, 78, 155.
335. Personal recourse to the sacrament of reconciliation: 29.
336. Love of the Church, Spouse of Christ: 29, 65, 155.

337. Pastoral charity: 29, 59, 63, 82.

338. Service of the least of the brothers, *attention to social needs:* 23, 81, 85-86, 153.

339. Devotion to Mary: 158.

340. Sacramental and realistic brotherhood: 50, 64, 151.

341. Permanent formation, study: 29, 151.

XLV — PRIESTLY VOCATION

342. *Call of the Church:* 23.

343. Call to be "friends" of Christ: 64.

344. *Call renewed each day:* 65.

XLVI — SECULAR INSTITUTES

345. *Marvelous flourishing:* 167.

346. Authentic consecration, lived in the world: 189.

347. Recognition by the Church: 189.

348. Specific vocation: 189.

349. *Common life not required:* 263.

JOHN PAUL II
SPEAKS TO RELIGIOUS

PRINCIPAL ALLOCUTIONS
AND LETTERS
1993-1994

1

TO CLOISTERED RELIGIOUS, IN ASSISI

January 10, 1993

1.   It is with great joy that, coming to Assisi to pray for peace in Europe together with my brothers in the episcopate, the representatives of the other Churches and Christian communities and others who believe in God, men and women of good will, I have wanted to visit you, gathered here in the Basilica of Saint Clare, in this city on a hillside, now a worldwide symbol of prayer and peace.

You represent the rich variety of women's Institutes of the contemplative life, united in the gift and commitment of religious consecration and the following of Christ; *you live in communion with the universal Church* and the Successor of Peter, *but you are profoundly inserted into the local Church,* gathered around your Ordinary, Bishop Sergio Goretti, whom I greet with affection. In this way you show your vocation to be living members of the diocesan family, to share in its joys and hopes, witnesses of the events which mark its history.

This inspiring moment of prayer, which finds gathered around the Pope the cloistered communities present in the diocese — the Poor Clares, the Capuchin Poor Clares, the Augustinians, and the Benedictines, is a foretaste here on earth of the communion of your saintly founders in heaven. Together with us, they are praying that the will of the Father, who wants peace for all his children, may be done "on earth as it is in heaven." Yes, this meeting of ours is an experience of the *"communio sanctorum"* in the charity and unity of the Father, Son and Holy Spirit.

2.   On this day of prayer for peace in Europe, how could I fail to remember with you in a special way the many religious living in those tormented regions of the Balkans, many of whom belong to the Franciscan family? They have offered, and continue to offer, their heroic witness of charity and are working for the reconciliation of hearts, sharing the difficulties and sufferings of the people, often risking their own lives.

You, dear Sisters, who belong to the communities of contemplative life in this diocese, are a living representation of all the places in Europe and the whole world where, day after day, and especially on this occasion, contemplatives are raising their persistent prayers to the Giver of all good things, so that the Spirit of love and forgiveness, of harmony and peace, may descend upon all. The world needs you to "pray, lifting up holy hands, without anger or argument" (cf. 1 Tm 2:8), imploring peace.

3.   You represent the Church, the Bride, the *"Ecclesia orans,"* who in her persevering and single-hearted prayer in the monasteries of the West joins in the ardent intercession of the monasteries of the East *"for the peace which comes from on high and for the unity of all"* (cf. *Prayer for peace in the Byzantine liturgy*).

Two saints are indissolubly linked in the memory of this city of Assisi: Francis and Clare. Two names, two vocations, which evoke the Gospel values of charity, poverty, purity, of spiritual friendship, prayer and peace. Here we are in the presence of the mortal remains of Saint Clare, in the protomonastery where her presence is felt and her ideal of holiness remains, lived by her many spiritual daughters all over the world today.

I am happy to be with you, dear Daughters of Saint Clare, on the threshold of the jubilee celebrations for the eight hundredth anniversary of her birth. It is a year of grace which will allow the entire community of believers to pause in admiration before the charism of this "evangelical woman" who radiates in a special way the mystery of Christ. Like Francis, Clare is a living image of the poor Christ. The most authentic disciple of the "Poverello," she liked to refer to herself as "Clare, the unworthy servant of Christ, and the little plant of the most blessed father Francis..." (*Rule of Saint Clare*, I, 3). Both of them expressed the primitive Franciscan ideal of the complementary nature of preaching the Gospel, done by Francis and his friars, and the contemplative life in poverty and penance embraced by Clare and her sisters. If it is true that Clare was a "reflection of Francis," and that in him "she saw herself completely, as in a mirror," there is no doubt that, in the communion of the same Spirit, the light of Clare's purity and poverty enlightened the countenance of the "Poverello," just as the memory of her and the certainty of her prayer enlightened his heart in times of difficulty and trial. For this reason Clare is indissolubly linked to Francis and the Gospel message of the two is complementary.

4.   Coming among you in March 1982, I urged you to prepare for and to celebrate with great solemnity the eighth centenary of the birth of your spiritual Mother. At that time I said to you: "In our age it is necessary to repeat Saint Clare's discovery, because it is important for the life of the Church. You do not know, hidden and unknown as you are, how important you are in the life of the Church, how many problems, how many things, depend on you. We need the rediscovery of that charism, of that vocation; we need the rediscovery of the divine legend of Francis and Clare" (March 12, 1982).

      On this occasion, when the eyes of Europe and the world are turned to Assisi, it seems that the message of Francis and Clare can be summed up in three ever timely evangelical words: *poverty, peace, prayer.*

5.   Following the example of Francis, Clare chose the
        path of Gospel poverty. She who invited Saint
Agnes of Prague "as a poor virgin (to) embrace the poor
Christ" (*Second Letter to Agnes of Prague*, n. 18), loved to
contemplate the Lord of glory in his poverty in order to
live out of love for him "who was placed poor in the crib,
lived poor in the world, and remained naked on the
cross" (*Testament*, n. 45). Indeed, she was aware that she
belonged to a "little flock" which "the Lord Father has
begotten in his holy Church by the word and example of
our blessed father Francis by following the poverty and
humility of his beloved Son and his glorious virgin
Mother" (*ibid.*, n. 46).

6.   *Poverty and peace,* then, are like the two faces of the
        mystery of Christ. They are two demands of
his message, as valid as ever for today's world in which
you, dear Sisters, are called to bear faithful Gospel
witness with your disarming poverty lived in the total
unity of meek and reconciled hearts. In *the Message for
this year's Day of Peace* I urged believers to *live the spirit of
Gospel poverty as a source of peace.* "Such evangelical
poverty," I wrote, "is the source of peace, since through
it the individual can establish a proper relationship with
God, with others and with creation" (n. 5).

7.   *However, there is no peace without prayer.* Every day
        the Church asks this gift of the Lord during
the Eucharistic celebration. When human hope of peace
seems to dissolve, when we feel even more strongly the
forces of evil and the influence of the evil one who, being
the "dia-bolos," the "separator," sows the spirit of hatred
and division in hearts, Christians, harmoniously united
in the name of Christ (cf. Mt 18: 19-20), persevere in
praying to the *"Most High, all powerful, good Lord,"*
invoking from him the Spirit of peace and goodness, the

Spirit who moves hearts and inspires thoughts of peace and not of affliction.

8.   For this very reason we have come to Assisi; we have also come to Assisi for your sake, *to ask God for peace*. The Pope wants to entrust this task to you, dear Sisters, that the sacred flame of prayer for peace may not die out, and the incense of prayer, together with the offering of the Body and Blood of Christ, will not cease rising to heaven.

I ask you to continue to support my universal *Petrine ministry* by the power of your unceasing prayer. Yes, by prayer which reveals itself to be a special aspect of the Church's *Marian* profile. Within the Church, in fact, you are a particular "icon" of the mystery of Mary, according to the words Francis addressed to Clare and her sisters.

Now, together with your Bishop, the Cardinals and the Bishops who are accompanying me, I want to offer you a blessing. It is a disinterested blessing, but in a certain sense it has a vested interest, knowing that you request the blessing and that in exchange you pray and fast more than the Pope does, much more than all of us. I am very happy to visit the tomb of Saint Francis as well as this shrine of his spiritual sister, Saint Clare. I am happy to meet you, to see that you have new vocations. I see all these white veils and the very young faces. I hope that you may always have vocations because we need this army equipped with prayer, sacrifice, poverty, humility, obedience and love.

9.   Like Saint Clare, in fact, "By divine inspiration you have made yourselves daughters and servants of the Most High King, the heavenly Father, and have taken the Holy Spirit as your Spouse, choosing to live according to the perfection of the holy Gospel" (*Writings to Clare at Assisi:* Forma vivendi, in RCI VI, 3).

Imitate Mary in her continual and fervent intercession. "Mary, as the *Catechism of the Catholic Church* reminds us, "is the perfect Orans (pray-er), a figure of the Church. When we pray to her, we are adhering with her to the plan of the Father, who sends his Son to save all men.... We can pray with and to her. The prayer of the Church is sustained by the prayer of Mary and united with it in hope" (n. 2679). Yes, on this occasion also, our prayer and our hopes for peace are sustained by Mary, *Regina Pacis, Spes nostra!* (...)

2

TO RELIGIOUS IN ROME

February 2, 1993

10. *"He came in the Spirit into the Temple"* (Lk 2:27).
The words which we read in the Gospel passage of today's liturgy refer to Simeon, a pious Israelite "awaiting the consolation of the Lord," that is, the coming of the Messiah.

To him was entrusted the word of Revelation at the moment of Jesus' presentation in the Temple of Jerusalem, forty days after his birth in Bethlehem. The evangelist points out that *the Holy Spirit was upon this righteous and devout man* (cf. Lk 2:25), to whom it had been revealed that "he should not see death before he had seen the Messiah of the Lord" (Lk 2:26). The evangelist particularly emphasizes that Simeon, moved by the Spirit, went to the Temple the day on which "the parents brought in the child Jesus to perform the custom of the Law in his regard" (Lk 2:27).

The Gospel passage presents togetherwith Simeon *the prophetess Anna*, thus underscoring her participation in the Revelation of the Messiah: "Coming forward at that very time, she gave thanks to God and spoke about the child to all who were awaiting the redemption of Jerusalem" (Lk 2:38).

11. *The presentation* of Jesus in the Temple of Jerusalem *is closely related to the mystery of the Epiphany*. In fact, Epiphany sheds greater light on the presence and action of the Holy Spirit, who leads people to meet and recognize the Savior and then bear witness to him.

The Holy Spirit will descend upon the Apostles on the day of Pentecost. At the time of the presentation his presence is an anticipation of and preparation for that day. It anticipates and prepares thirty years in advance, his manifestation on the banks of the Jordan and the whole messianic mission of Jesus of Nazareth.

At the same time, Jesus' presentation in the Temple dramatically expresses the manner of his salvific mission. Addressing Mary, the Mother of Jesus, Simeon says: "*He is* destined for the fall and rise of many in Israel, and to be *a sign that will be contradicted* so that the thoughts of many hearts may be revealed" (Lk 2:34-35).

12.   Enlightened by the Holy Spirit, Simeon sees in the Child presented to God by Mary and Joseph the One who has come to take care of the children of Abraham. "Therefore he had to become like his brothers in every way, that he might be a merciful and faithful *high priest* before God to expiate the sins of the people" (Heb 2:17).

But does Simeon see all this? Does the prophetess Anna truly see it? *The Church, however, finds all this in their testimony.* She finds it in the words of Simeon.

In them the Church also finds a spiritual reference to that Temple whose gates lift up their lintels so that the king of glory may enter (cf. Ps 24[23]:7); he who, at the same time, is a sign of contradiction.

13.   Dear brothers and sisters, in this solemn celebration of the feast of the Presentation of the Lord in the Temple, I cordially greet all of you who have come here, led by the Holy Spirit, on the path of vocation and consecration. It joins you in a special way to Christ, the King of glory. To Christ, the sign of contradiction, obedient unto death, poor and chaste. To Christ, Son of the Virgin.

I greet you who are part of the Church of Rome, built upon the foundation of Peter and Paul, upon the foundation of the apostles and the prophets. I address you, *brothers and sisters* belonging to *the many families of the religious and monastic life living in Rome* and, together with you and through you, I address all consecrated persons throughout *the whole world*.

Today's liturgy, in which the Church gives glory to Christ, "a light for revelation to the Gentiles" (Lk 2:32), is in a special way, your liturgy and your day. It is also an occasion of great joy for the bishop of Rome, who on this day has the opportunity to meet you and to *thank* the Lord *for the gift of the consecrated life, of religious life, to the Church.*

14. As the Second Vatican Council strongly emphasized, religious life is *a great gift for the Church's mission in the world* and makes a valuable contribution not only to the many pastoral activities, but especially to the variety of charisms and the witness of total fidelity that it must give to the Gospel. Unfailingly, "the profession of the evangelical counsels, then, appears as a sign which can and ought to attract all the members of the Church to an effective and prompt fulfillment of the duties of their Christian vocation." (*Lumen gentium*, n. 44).

Our century has not failed to produce *eminent witnesses* of such a radical living out of the Gospel. During the past year I had the joy of raising a considerable number of consecrated persons to the honors of the altar. Some of those people had offered their faithful Gospel witness with the *supreme sacrifice of their life*. I am thinking, for example, of the Claretian martyrs of Barbastro, an entire religious community composed of priests, theology students who were close to ordination, and lay brothers who were executed in Spain in 1936. These heroic heralds of Christ died with the crucifix clasped in their hands.

15.   Bands of humble, often hidden disciples of the
       Lord have continued to follow them on the path
of martyrdom, and are still doing so. How could we fail
to make mention here of the missionaries who have died
in the field of evangelization and missionary activity?
How could we fail to recall the consecrated souls,
silently immolated on the altar of total self-giving to
God? Their example, their blood poured out, is *the seed
of new vocations*.

       While some areas of the world unfortunately
continue to experience a worrisome vocational winter,
in other places, where adherence to the Gospel is more
confident and courageous, an authentic spring time is
under way, rich in hope and promise for the Church and
humanity. The Spirit of the Lord acts with all the more
power when consecrated persons and the whole Christian family are more decisive in refusing to adapt to the
spirit of this world and more generous in accepting the
mystery of the Cross.

16.   The hoped-for renewal of the community of be-
       lievers and *authentic ecumenism*, so intimately
linked to the new evangelization, can find a valid support and an irreplaceable contribution in the faithful
practice of the evangelical counsels. We truly need, as
we reflected during the recent Week of Prayer for
Christian Unity, to "bear the fruit of the Spirit for
Christian unity." This will take place above all thanks to
your daily immolation, dear brothers and sisters, called
to follow the Lord in the consecrated life. The Church
is counting on you!

       With confidence, therefore, let us invoke God,
certain that in our day too, so afflicted by a spirit which
is opposed to the truth brought by Christ, he will not fail
to give the Church holy and courageous persons totally
consecrated to the glory of God and the true good of

their brothers and sisters, shining witnesses of the Gospel message.

17.   Dear men and women religious, *this is your day*.
    In each of you, and in your religious families, the Church sees *the continuous action of the Holy Spirit*. You too, moved by the Holy Spirit, enter the Temple: the great spiritual space which is the Church of God; you enter it to be a living witness, a prophecy of the kingdom of God in the midst of the people of our day.

    How providential were the prophetic words of Simeon and Anna spoken on this fortieth day after Jesus' birth.

    How *blessed is your witness*, your prophecy of life and mission every day!

    Dear brothers and sisters, be sharers of the Light "that shines in the darkness" (Jn 1, 5). Serve Christ, the Light of the World.

    May our eyes see the light of salvation which God has prepared in the sight of all the nations.

    Like the prudent virgins in the Gospel parable, may you be watchful as you await the Bridegroom, in order to run out to meet him, with your lamps burning, when he comes. Amen!

3

TO PRIESTS, RELIGIOUS, SEMINARIANS AND LAITY IN COTONOU, BENIN

February 4, 1993

18.　"God chose to make known the riches of the glory of this mystery among the Gentiles; it is Christ in you, the hope for glory" (Col 1:27).

I joyfully repeat these words of the apostle Paul which we heard during evening prayer in your cathedral. Priests, women and men religious, committed lay faithful, representing all the dioceses of Benin, we give thanks: "Christ is among you."

I thank you for your warm reception. I thank Bishop Monsi-Agboka for his words of welcome. Yes, we want to *give thanks* because, following the first ancient contact with Christianity, *the Church has really taken root in your land* since 1861, when Fathers Borghero and Fernandez arrived here after one of their companions had already given his life, joining in the "suffering of Christ." Among so many Gospel workers, I should like to pay homage to the first bishops, Bishops Dartois, Steinmetz and Parisot: they strengthened the building of the Church and entrusted it to the sons of Benin who soon followed them in the priesthood and then in the episcopate. I am thinking of the bishop whom Pope Paul VI subsequently called to Rome, Cardinal Gantin, present here with me, as well as of the bishops of your six dioceses who are gathered here.

19.　Through the delegates who fill this cathedral, I would like to *encourage all the ecclesial communities in Benin in their fidelity to the Gospel*, as Saint Paul did: "Persevere in the faith, firmly grounded, stable, and not shifting from the hope of the Gospel that you received" (Col 1:23). These words are addressed to *lay people, to catechists, to the vice-presidents of pastoral councils, to those in charge of organizations and movements.* By their witness and service, they have played a considerable role in the development and vitality of the Church in this land. Their activity remains fundamental for the people of God. Dear lay friends, continue to serve your parishes and dioceses with the faith and generosity that were a great gift from the Lord during the difficult years. However, do not forget either that you are the first to be able to bring the Gospel spirit to your work environment, to all the classes of society, for the demanding tasks of rebuilding your country. It is the duty of lay Christians, by their skill, righteousness and impartiality, to be the true artisans of the common good, in unison with all their people.

20.   Saint Paul tells us that he wants to proclaim Christ, "teaching everyone with all wisdom, that we may present everyone perfect in Christ" (Col 1:28). The aim of evangelization could not be better expressed: "to present everyone perfect in Christ." This means *accepting God's gifts* in one's innermost core, and *nurturing one's spiritual life.* Such an appeal equally concerns those who are committed to the priesthood or to religious life, as well as the lay faithful. No one could feel responsible in the Church without constantly striving to draw inspiration and strength from the sources of prayer: the Word of God, the Liturgy of the Hours, the sacraments, which are essential encounters with the Lord in his redeeming grace, and most particularly the Eucharist, through which the ecclesial community is established. May all individuals, each according to the demands of their own vocation, let themselves be drawn to the Lord in heart-to-heart prayer. May they be guided by the Mother of Jesus, who treasured the wonders of

salvation in her heart! May everyone seek to accept the Good News and share it as their most valuable treasure, in the family, in the community, and with their brothers and sisters who do not yet know it!

21. *Religious*, you have a specific role in evangelization, for you are called to be witnesses committed without reserve. I give thanks for the flourishing of religious vocations in this country, and also for the good cooperation between those who came from other parts of the world since the earliest days of missionary activity and the people of Benin, who in turn have answered the Lord's call in the various local and international institutes. Living according to the different charisms of your Orders and Congregations, *you show the way of this "perfection in Christ"* for which we all must strive, after the example of Saint Paul; your vocation leads you to *total self-giving for the sake of the Kingdom of God*, and makes you witnesses, for your brothers and sisters, of the courageous commitment of a whole life to following Christ. You play your part in *the different forms of evangelical service*: the service of praise and intercession is the priority of *monastic life*, so firmly rooted in Benin. For your daily pastoral tasks, for education, for the care of the sick and the poor, the *apostolic religious* are irreplaceable leaders and good examples. Continue your activities with the generosity of your consecration to the Lord, and be aware of the respect that Peter's successor and his brothers in the episcopate have for you. I would also like to add that African religious, remembering that religious life in its monastic form was born on their continent, can contribute a great deal to their brothers and sisters of other regions of the world because of the freshness of their commitment and their detachment from material things, as well as the simplicity of their life: may they know that the whole Church is counting on them!

22.   And you, *the priests*, together with your bishops, truly assure the existence of the Church by the multiple forms of your ministry that we celebrated yesterday during the ordination. Thanks be to God, *Beninese priests* are now the most numerous in the country, whereas the first Dahomeans ordained have already entered the peace of the kingdom. I sincerely encourage you with affection and trust: your task is difficult but exalting: for the people of God, you are the *stewards of gifts, guides and teachers in the faith*. This requires from you first an ever renewed faithfulness in the love of the Lord and of your neighbor: *live celibacy as an essential sign* of your availability to serve, your renunciation and your freedom with regard to material possessions as well as to human prestige. Be the loyal coworkers of the bishops, and yourselves collaborate with lay people in a spirit of openness and respect. We are in the cathedral of Our Lady of Mercy; this serves to remind us that your *ministry should be one of mercy*, consolation, peacemaking, unity. With your whole being you are signs of the vivifying and liberating presence of the Savior.

23.   Much of what I have just said also applies to you, the *seminarians*. It is a joy for me to see so many of you, the lovely community of Ouidah — the seminary which, unfortunately, I am unable to visit — with your friends in the propaedeutic year and the younger ones who are in the minor seminaries. Seminarians, you are undergoing a period of formation and especially of discernment: in dialogue with the formation staff, sustained by community life and by your intimacy with the Lord in meditation and prayer, *seek the truth of your vocation*. Be fully disposed to accepting the call of the Church: it is she who through the bishop will authenticate your vocation. Be ready to make the gift of yourselves, and it must be said, to make sacrifices: with the

staunch generosity of youth, be sensitive to the needs of your brothers and sisters, starting with the most deprived; prepare yourselves to be with them, like the Lord, poor in the eyes of the world and rich in the gifts of God that will be entrusted to you to transmit to them. Be ready to resist many temptations and to bear your part of human suffering, as Saint Paul said, "on behalf of (Christ's) Body, the Church" (Col 1:24). Then you will hear the Lord say to you, "Well done, my good and faithful servant.... Come and share your master's joy" (Mt 25:23).

24.   *Some representatives of other ecclesial communities* have wanted to join us this evening. I would like to thank you for your presence and I greet you cordially. I firmly hope that you will *continue your exchanges and your common prayer* with your Catholic brothers and sisters. It is good to get together to hear the Word of God, in order to be the most credible witnesses in the world. It is also useful to come together *to put real evangelical charity into practice*. May the Lord bless your ecumenical actions!

25.   Dear friends, priests, men and women religious and lay faithful, your spiritual and pastoral experience is going to *contribute to the reflections of the Synod of Bishops for Africa*. I ask you to pray that the sessions may be fruitful and stimulating for the mission of evangelization entrusted to the Church on this continent. Your gathering is already a sign of hope. I hope that each of you may always respond better to your own vocation and may be able to say of your labor, like the apostle Paul, that you have done it "with the strength of Christ's power working within me" (Col 1:29). In the name of the Lord, I wholeheartedly impart my blessing to you.

4

TO PRIESTS, RELIGIOUS AND SEMINARIANS IN KAMPALA, UGANDA

February 9, 1993

26.   It is with "joy inspired by the Holy Spirit" (1 Thes 1:6) that we gather in this cathedral of the archdiocese of Kampala for the opening session of the *Council of the General Secretariat of the Synod of Bishops for the Special Assembly for Africa*(...)

With deep affection in our Lord Jesus Christ, I wish to greet the representatives of the *priests, men and women religious, and seminarians of the dioceses of Uganda* who are with us this evening. Through you, dear brothers and sisters in Christ, we are able to pay tribute to all who work to bring the Gospel to those for whom the Good Shepherd laid down his life. It is indeed fitting that you should be here with bishops from all over Africa, for you remind us of the hopes and expectations that so many people have for this Special Assembly.

27.   You are the workers whom the Lord is sending into the harvest to make ready the "great springtime of Christianity" (*Redemptoris missio*, n. 86) which he is preparing for his Church! The *abundance of vocations* to the priesthood and consecrated life in Uganda reveals the Church's vitality and fervor — a gift for which we must give thanks and praise to God!

This vigorous evangelizing effort would be impossible without the courageous men and women who, impelled by the love of Christ (cf. 2 Cor 5:14), have been coming to this land for over a century on the mission *ad gentes*. I make my own the tribute of my beloved predecessor Pope Paul VI, who wrote:

28.　"The action of the *missionaries* was always disinterested and animated by the charity of the Gospel, and (...) in order to help the African peoples to resolve the complex human and social problems in their countries, they spent themselves generously" (*Africae terrarum*, n. 24). Esteemed brothers and sisters, you are heirs of a great tradition — a heritage shaped by the grace so powerfully at work in the White Fathers, the Mill Hill Fathers, the sons and daughters of Bishop Comboni, and all members of missionary Congregations. Convinced that the Gospel is "the power of God for salvation" (Rom 1:16), these men and women came here out of love for the people of Uganda, a love which has been heroically confirmed in recent years by your standing faithfully with your people in times of trial.

In you we see that the *Church's mission to evangelize is not for a season past but is forever valid* (cf. *Redemptoris missio*, n. 66). Do not count the cost of being servants of Christ and his Gospel (cf. 1 Cor 4:1). Never grow weary of extending the boundaries of the Kingdom of God. How blessed you will be to see, as Father Lourdel did, the mystery of Christ's dying and rising lived out in those you bring to the Lord.

29.　*Dear brother priests*, I address to you a word of heartfelt affection. You are the chief coworkers of your bishops in fulfilling the apostolic ministry handed on in the sacrament of Holy Orders (cf. *Presbyterorum ordinis*, n. 2). By your sacramental consecration you have been configured "to Jesus Christ as Head and Shepherd of the Church" (*Pastores dabo vobis*, n. 21). You continue our Savior's own mission of sacrificial love for his Bride, the Church, for whom he gave up his life (cf. Eph 5:25). This *pastoral charity* requires you to make a total gift of yourselves to the Church — a gift which you renew daily in offering the Eucharistic sacrifice (cf. *ibid.*, n. 23). And as you well know, your effectiveness as ministers of Christ's reconciling love and as preachers of the Gospel of conversion will be increased by frequent reception of the sacrament of Penance.

I urge you, as Saint Paul exhorted Timothy his beloved son and brother in the faith, "to rekindle the gift of God that is within you" (cf. 2 Tm 1:6). The dynamism of pastoral charity needs to be constantly rejuvenated and nourished by the God who makes all things new (cf. Rv 21:5). Participation in programs of permanent formation are means by which the Spirit leads you to an "ever deeper knowledge of the mystery of Christ... and of the mystery of Christian priesthood" (*Pastores dabo vobis*, n. 70). In such experiences you will gain the strength to persevere in your service to the flock. In this respect the National Diocesan Clergy Renewal Center here in Kampala will surely be of great service to the whole Church in Eastern Africa.

30.   Dear *seminarians*, you who are aspiring to take your place alongside the priests as workers in the Lord's vineyard, to you I extend the embrace of a loving father. Prepare yourselves well for the priceless gift that you will receive from God through "the laying on of hands." In order to grow into the "stature of the fullness of Christ" (cf. Eph 4:13), you must give yourselves completely to the program of spiritual, academic and pastoral formation set forth by those entrusted with your education. Do not waste a moment. In the time between now and your ordination day, you must diligently study the faith handed down to us by the apostles, and allow yourselves to be fashioned by the Holy Spirit into fitting vessels for this treasure (cf. 2 Cor 4:7). Through prayer, "form the habit of drawing close to Jesus as a friend" (cf. *Optatam totius*, n. 8), so that God's grace may bear abundant fruit in you (cf. Jn 15:8).

31.	Dear *men and women religious*, it is a cause of great
	joy that this land, made fruitful by the martyrs'
blood, has favored the growth of religious life. In
addition to the older Congregations which have found
a home here, the establishment of *flourishing new Institutes* is a clear sign of the growing maturity of the Church
in Uganda. Indeed, all of you are in some sense "sons
and daughters" of Saint Charles Lwanga and his companions. By the vows of chastity, poverty and obedience,
you as religious, like the martyrs, bear witness to the
truth that "the People of God has no lasting city here
below, but looks forward to one which is to come"
(*Lumen gentium*, n. 44). Called to be signs of the new
world of the future resurrection (cf. *Familiaris consortio*,
n. 16), you evangelize above all by offering your lives to
Christ as a "gift" (cf. *Perfectae caritatis*, n. 1), and making
manifest to all the new life won for us by the Cross.

	The witness of self-giving is borne not only by the
members of Institutes of active life but also by those
whose lives of silent contemplative love burn at the heart
of the Church — the Carmelites, Poor Clares,
Cistercians, Benedictines and the Sisters of Perpetual
Adoration. To all of you, men and women religious, I
repeat the invitation which I made in my Apostolic
Exhortation *Redemptionis donum*: "Renew your religious consecration according to the model of the consecration of the Mother of God" (n. 17). Like Mary, place
all that you are and all that you have in the Father's
hands (cf. Lk 1:38).

32.	Since religious life is a powerful instrument for
	spreading the light of Gospel truth, I wish to call
attention once again to the importance of the example
given by *women religious*, especially for missionary
Churches. In the lives of religious Sisters, "virginity for
the sake of the Kingdom is transformed into a mother-
hood in the spirit that is rich and fruitful" (*Redemptoris*

missio, n. 70). They show that the *vocation of every woman* — not only those in consecrated life, but also those in the married state — is to make a sincere "gift of self" to another. This truth about "the being of woman" — that she is a person created for self-giving to another person — is the basis for the respect rightly accorded her and for the role she is to play in the family and civil society (cf. *Mulieris dignitatem*, nn. 7, 21). (...)

5

LETTER TO THE ABBOT GENERAL OF THE ORDER OF CANONS REGULAR OF PREMONTRE

May 7, 1993

33.   In the long line of religious who have evangelized Europe and formed its cultural patrimony, the Order of Canons Regular of Prémontré occupies a privileged place. On Christmas night 1121, in the solitude of Prémontré, Saint Norbert gave birth to a new community of the ancient canonical Order, whose branches rapidly extended to Central Europe. In the wake of my predecessor, Pope Saint Gregory VII, Saint Norbert communicated to his sons an apostolic spirit, the fruits of which the Church reaps today on five continents.

During this year, 1993, your Order is celebrating the 850th anniversary of the official arrival of Norbertines in Bohemia, and the beginning of their work of evangelization in the heart of Europe. This Jubilee will be celebrated in the entire Order, but especially in the five abbeys of Strahov, Teplá, Zeliv, Nová Rise and Jasov, whose communities are now well on their way to re-establishment. With respect and admiration I acknowledge the religious who, during more than forty-five years of dispersion and persecution, did not hesitate to witness to their faith in Christ and their fidelity to the Holy See, often risking their lives. Far from being in vain, their sacrifice has been the source of new vocations.

At the eve of the third millennium, the insight of Saint Norbert still remains relevant. The re-establishment of your communities in Central Europe goes hand in hand with the new evangelization of the continent and the world. The new spirit which animates you makes you heralds of the Gospel of the risen Christ, that Good News which gives life its meaning and effects true liberty. In imitation of your holy Founder, forge new paths so that the Gospel message may penetrate hearts, mentalities, customs, cultures and so that those peoples now freed of oppression may receive Christ the Savior. Animated by this spirit, you will furnish society with the indispensable elements for its renewal, you will re-awaken the memory and the conscience of Europe and you will contribute to the building up of the civilization of Love.

34.   It is my wish that this Jubilee be for you and for all the Norbertine Order a time of renewal and a point of departure for a new apostolic fruitfulness. In order that this come about, draw from the treasury of your spiritual patrimony, live the charism of Saint Norbert, renew your fidelity to your Profession. In restoring your ancient and venerable abbeys, be concerned first of all to restore the communities of prayer and apostolate, which for more than eight centuries, were the source of an outstanding fruitfulness.

Saint Norbert and his first disciples expressed their ideal in the canonical formula of profession which is still yours today. They wished to put into practice the *Evangelica institutio* and to preach the Gospel, having renounced the goods of this world, as the Lord commanded the Apostles to do. The goal of your Order is more than ever relevant. Devote all your strength to it, with the intrepid courage which Christ alone can give you. People of our time have often lost their point of reference. The crisis of values leaves them unprepared in the face of the new challenges with which the rapid evolution of our society confronts them. By word and the witness of your personal and communal life, communicate to them the love of Christ and the Church.

35.   Faithful to the *Apostolica institutio,* your predecessors sought to make each of your Norbertine communities an image of the primitive community of Jerusalem, gathered around the Apostles and the Virgin Mary. By the profession of the evangelical counsels and your vow of stability, you consecrate yourselves for the service of your abbatial church, in order to solemnly celebrate the sacred Liturgy, to raise to God the praise of the entire Church, and to gather the Christian people around their Lord. May your abbeys, your priories, your parishes and your monasteries of nuns continue to fulfill this mission, so that God's Name may be glorified in all hearts and our contemporaries may find in you welcome, availability and apostolic zeal. May your abbeys be houses of prayer and schools of faith, opened to all of good will.

36.   In founding the Premonstratensian community, Saint Norbert chose the *Rule of Saint Augustine.* The first recommendations of this Rule underline the essential characteristic of your communities: "*The first purpose for which you have come together is to live in unity in the monastery and to be of one mind and one heart on the way to God*" (I, 2). The Augustinian community is founded on the love of God and the desire to know him better in order to love him better. It demands simplicity of heart and mutual love, fraternal assistance and unity of minds in the pursuit of that which alone is necessary.

37.   The Eucharist is the source of this charity and the goal of every apostolate. This explains why it was the wish of Saint Norbert that at the heart of every Norbertine community, the Eucharist would form the apex of the entire conventual life. The Norbertine abbot Philippe de Bonne-Espérance reminds us: "*In order that the Church not perish during the difficulties of the journey, she finds invaluable assistance by keeping watch over one of her*

65

treasures, the salvific sacrament of the Body of Christ; yet while it seems that it is the Church maintaining this treasure, it is rather this treasure which preserves the Church" (PL, 203:669).

38.   With Saint Norbert, who was a loving son of the Virgin Mary, entrust the renewal of your communities, the vocations to your Order, every one of your apostolates, and the entire Church to the Mother of the Redeemer. May Mary, who first received the Word in order to give it to the world, transform your communities into vital centers of the new evangelization.

While associating myself in a special way with the Norbertines of Central Europe on this occasion of their Jubilee, I express once more the trust and affection of the successor of Peter to the entire Order and to each of you and sincerely bestow upon you my apostolic blessing.

6

TO POOR CLARES IN CALTANISSETTA, ITALY

May 10, 1993

39.   I greet all of you with affection and turn my cordial thoughts to all of your Sisters who are not present at this meeting today, but who are certainly united with us in spirit. I am happy that my stop at this monastery dedicated to Saint Clare, your Mother and model, takes place at the very beginning of my pastoral visit to the Church of Caltanissetta. Thank you for your presence and your welcome; thanks, in particular, to Mother Gemma Ganci who, as President of the Federation of Poor Clare Monasteries of this island, has expressed cordial words of welcome in the name of all of you, recalling also that this year the Order is solemnly celebrating the eighth centenary of the birth of your holy Foundress. This is also an important occasion for the universal Church and for the Pope.

This happy anniversary makes my meeting with you all the more significant. In fact, in recalling her who was the first of the spiritual daughters of Saint Francis, I am pleased to underscore *the importance of the witness of consecrated life for our era*, a prophetic sign of the primacy of God over all things. Through your total gift to God, dear Sisters, you are called to offer the Church a constant reminder that, as the community of the risen Lord, she should seek "what is above, where Christ is seated at the right hand of God" (Col 3:1). Monasteries, *veritable oases of the spirit*, where "the better part... (which) will not be taken away" (Lk 10:42) is chosen as the primary motive of life, thus become silent schools of evangelical life, capable of spurring believers to live for God in all the concrete conditions of their life.

Quite willingly, therefore, I entrust to your hands raised in prayer the steps of this my apostolic pilgrimage and my mission in the Church and the world. Support me with your dedication so that I may always "strengthen the brothers" in accordance with Christ's command (cf. Lk 22:32).

40.   From this place which is in a certain sense the heart of the diocesan community, I want to thank you for the hidden service you give to the cause of the Gospel, to the spread of the Kingdom of God among humanity. *Yours is an essential role in the apostolate of the ecclesial community*: like lamps burning continually before the altar of the Lamb, you support the activity of all those who are involved on the many frontiers of evangelization. May the Lord make you more conscious, day after day, of this your mission. Continue on this journey of holiness and fidelity to the Gospel with constancy and joy, with docility to the Holy Spirit and missionary zeal, listening to God and in fraternal communion of hearts.

During this eighth centenary of the birth of Saint Clare, addressing all the Poor Clares spread throughout so many parts of Sicily, I would like to offer for your meditation some thoughts taken from her testament. Your holy Mother wrote as follows: "Among the gifts that we have received and do daily receive from our benefactor, the Father of mercies, and for which we must glorify him with lively acts of thanksgiving, the greatest is that of our vocation" ("Testament," n. 2).

To give thanks for the gift of a vocation means to love the divine call; to love it means to live it, to live it in its fullness means to give it to your brothers and sisters like a fire which spreads.

What is this gift of vocation to which your holy Foundress recalls her daughters, but the mystery of the nuptial love of Christ, given through the Spirit to each of you? Dear Sisters, you belong to Christ alone, and are called to live always for him in an attitude of daily oblation which places you in constant communion with the joyful and sad events of the Church. Your vocation is love, not a love which imprisons in the close confines of the cloister, but which *enlarges your hearts to the very ends of the earth*. You live for Christ: therefore you live for the Church.

The cloistered life is prophetic. Living exclusively for the Lord in the bonds of poverty, obedience and chastity, you are invited to show people that God alone is the genuine wealth capable of fulfilling every human desire. Dependence on him is the condition for true and lasting peace of heart. Consecrated in absolute fidelity to Christ, you can thus sing before all of humanity the joy of those who see God (cf. Mt 5:8), proclaiming in time the mystery of that eternal day in which God will "be all in all" (1 Cor 15:28). Here we have Saint Francis' "Canticle of the Creatures," open to the vision of God.

41.   Saint Clare writes again: "I commend all my Sisters, both those present and those to come, to our holy Mother the Roman Church, to the Supreme Pontiff (...) that out of love of the Lord who, born in poverty, was placed in the crib, lived poorly in the world, and remained naked on the cross, (he) may always see to it that his little flock ... observe the holy poverty that we have promised to God and our most blessed father Saint Francis" ("Testament," nn. 44-47).

Imitate the poor and crucified Christ: this is the Franciscan ideal of which you must be an example and living message. It is a model of Christian life which the *Poverello* of Assisi chose as his emblem, a model that is still valid today, in a world in which people frequently believe they can find the source of happiness in wealth and in acquiring material goods.

How much humanity needs your witness, which will lead it to think about the true values, which are not subject to the wear and tear of time! How much it needs your serenity, which springs from your intimate union with Christ! Dear Sisters, continue to be faithful daughters of Saint Francis and Saint Clare.

Joyful poverty, love for the crucified, the total gift of yourself without fear or hesitation are the most valuable contributions which you can make to the new evangelization. Faithful to your holy Rule, every monastery will appear as the evangelical city set on the mountaintop (cf. Mt 5:14), towards which tired travelers raise their eyes in order to find faith and hope on their journey.

With these wishes, and entrusting you to the protection of Mary, of your Founders, of all your saints and blessed — there are so many of them in this family, a wealth of holiness produced over the centuries — I gladly impart to all those present and to all the Poor Clares, especially the elderly and infirm, my apostolic blessing.

7

TO THE INTERNATIONAL UNION OF SUPERIORS GENERAL, IN ROME

May 14, 1993

42. I am happy to welcome you, dear Sisters, to this meeting which takes place during the assembly of the International Union of Superiors General (UISG).(...)

The theme of your convention is very rich in meaning: *"Apostolic women religious at the service of life."* It is a topic that reveals your identity of consecration and mission in the Church and opens up to you new prospects for a re-evangelization of society in our day. Commitment to life is rooted in him who is "the Life" (Jn 14:6), who came that all "might have life and have it more abundantly" (Jn 10:10).

"It was not you who chose me, but I who chose you" (Jn 15:6), Jesus said to his Apostles in the Upper Room before his passion. He repeats these words to you too, inviting you to a specific service within the Church. Each of you can legitimately feel called by name, looked upon with a special predilection by the divine Master. "I chose you... to go...": Christ's statement explains quite well how, in your situation as apostolic women religious, *vocation is for mission.*

43. Like the women who accompanied the Lord during his preaching, to Calvary and beyond death, in order to be the first to proclaim his resurrection, you too are called by the special bond of your consecration to be *living witnesses of the Gospel.* Therefore, in the variety of its charisms, the apostolic religious life for women is given to the Church so that, as the Bride of Christ, she may fully express her own mission

of grace and bear witness to all of the "inscrutable riches of Christ" (Eph 3:8).

In reality religious life is rooted in the joyful confession of Jesus' Resurrection and in the conviction and personal adherence to the risen Christ in order to be a credible proclamation in the world of his presence, of God's love which is stronger than death and sin, of the glorious destiny of our life.

44.   The theme of your Assembly arouses in me feelings, hopes and desires which I would like to express to you today, dear Sisters, actively involved in the specific sector of the "Gospel of life." By their virginal consecration and the apostolic charisms stirred up by the Spirit, women religious have always been near to the problems of life: at the side of children, the infirm, the elderly, the poor, the dying, in helping unwed mothers, in education, catechesis, and a thousand fields of missionary activity.

Today such social problems *have become more acute and complex.* In many situations humanity seems to have lost the sense of the sacredness of life. We need only think of the continuing fratricidal wars, the offenses against the dignity of defenseless women, the exploitation of innocent children, and the many attacks against the human being. A civilization which exalts the values of the person without, however, rooting that value in the truth inscribed in consciences and revealed by Christ, falls into the contradiction of denying the right to life, especially to the most innocent and defenseless.

45.   Your special vocation, marked by courageous choices adapted to the needs of the Church and the world, must be expressed on the frontiers of the defense of human life throughout its earthly duration, from conception to its natural completion. However, *an authentic defense of life requires the proclamation of the*

Gospel and, as a consequence, teaching universal brotherhood in Christ, the promotion of human rights, the defense of woman and her dignity, a culture of peace and communion among peoples, respect for creation, the gift of God which should lead people to bless and praise the Creator. Your total and exclusive consecration is already a witness to the value of existence which has its beginning and end in God. We are born for life, for immortal life.

46.   Dear Sisters, be present with love and prophetic dedication wherever life is endangered, threatened, offended, mocked; wherever it requires special care. *To serve life is to give life*, as Jesus' example shows us. Here is the secret of an apostolic life that cannot fail to be rooted in a great love which, consecrated to God, day after day dedicates itself to bearing witness to him to our neediest neighbors. It is a love which grows with communion, is deepened by sharing, expands in planning and fulfilling the mission. It is a love which sometimes, like that of Jesus, ends up as an effective offering of one's own existence as well.

47.   How many apostolic women religious belonging to your Institutes have sealed their total dedication to the Lord and their service to the weak and abandoned *with the grace of martyrdom!* May their example be a stimulus and support for you. It is worth living one's consecration fully when day after day it becomes total self-giving, an expression of that "greatest" love which makes us like Christ.

In order for your mission to respond effectively to the expectations of the particular historical moment in which we live, it is necessary *to give new life to your charism and to fidelity to the evangelical counsels* through a constant spiritual renewal, "which must always be

assigned primary importance even in the active ministry" (*Perfectae caritatis,* n. 2).

48.   Trust in him who has called you and chosen you.
      He says words of courage and hope to you: *"It was
not you who chose me, but I who chose you"* (Jn 15:16).
Respond to today's religious and social challenges *with
an intense interior life, a deeper, more living prayer, a real
spirit of sacrifice and renunciation of the world's mentality,*
united in heart and generous in giving witness. Most of
all, have *a great love for Christ in the sacrament of the
Eucharist.* His Spirit will fan into a flame within you the
fire of divine charity, renewing a type of "Pentecost of
the consecrated life." He will make you capable of
conveying the message of life incisively and effectively.
This is my desire and prayer for you, in view also of the
coming Synod on the consecrated life and its mission in
the Church and the world. (...)

8

TO PRIESTS, RELIGIOUS AND LAY LEADERS IN AREZZO, ITALY

May 23, 1993

49.   Great is my joy over this meeting, which sees the priests, religious, seminarians, catechists, members of the pastoral councils, parish councils, and the diocesan council, and representative of the lay movements and groups gathered in the cathedral, the spiritual heart of the diocese. You are the chosen portion of this Church of Arezzo-Cortona-Sansepolcro, a particular Church with its own characteristics, as Vatican II showed us in *Lumen gentium*, called as you are, in various roles and responsibilities, to serve more closely the cause of the proclamation of the Gospel (...).

I want to express to each and every one my appreciation and affection. I want to echo the sentiments of Christ himself, the Good Shepherd. He is in our midst, and he asks us to believe firmly in his promise: "Behold, I am with you always, to the end of the age" (Mt 28:20).

This certitude gives us consolation and hope. And we really need it during this time of growing difficulty for apostolic activity and for faith itself, so exposed to indifference, and often even to open hostility. Is it perhaps not true that sometimes we feel tired and discouraged, just like Jesus' disciples on Lake Genesareth, and we are tempted to give in to discouragement? "We have worked hard all night and have caught nothing!" (Lk 5:5).

However, nothing is lost if in the hour of darkness we are able to trust once again in him, Jesus, in whom we have placed our joy and hope. The success of our apostolate depends on the tenor of our faith. We must be able to confess with the zeal of Paul: "What will separate us from the love of Christ? Will anguish, or distress, or persecution, or famine, or nakedness, or peril, or the sword?" (Rom 8:35). Yes, dear brothers and sisters, it is time to cry out with all the strength of our hearts: nothing "will be able to separate us from the love of Christ" (Rom 8:39). This is the most authentic, Pauline, apostolic expression of what the source of our strength is, was, and will be.

50. Dear priests, it is first to you that I express my affectionate greeting. Together with the bishop, you bear the daily burden of pastoral care in this Church to which you have consecrated your life entirely.

However, I know how complex and difficult your service has become for many reasons, including the decline in the number of vocations. While pastoral demands are growing, the forces are dwindling, or at least seem to be diminishing because, taking into consideration the figures for the whole Church, they are no longer decreasing but are actually increasing. There is a difficulty, a difficulty matched by others concerning the life of the priest, especially when he is tried by old age, illness and solitude. Who would be surprised if this causes some bitterness and even tempts people to discouragement?

More timely than ever is the Lord's invitation to a heartfelt, insistent prayer that he "send workers into the harvest" (Mt 9:38), not just in Korea, or India, or Africa, but in Italy, too, in Arezzo, in Europe too. And this is timely for the priests as well as for the religious Congregations, for the convents, for this very valuable apostolate performed by the sisters of the apostolic Congregations. I am glad to see that you are moving in that direction through the "Year of Vocations" which will conclude on the feast of the Immaculate Conception. May the Lord and the Blessed Virgin listen to the prayer which ascends from the whole diocese and enflame the hearts of so many children and young adults for the sublime ideal of the ministerial priesthood.

However, we do well not to forget that God's call also comes through our generous, joyous witness. Only a priesthood lived with enthusiasm can serve as an ideal for a young man, especially in an age such as ours, so filled with empty pleasures. Therefore, be at the side of the young, helping them to discover their vocation in the Church and in society. Offer them your personal witness, and the example of your priestly fraternity, growing in mutual esteem, in cooperation with one another and with your Pastor, who will not fail to be at your side and support you in your daily efforts. May fraternity always be your joy and the support of your apostolic activity.

This priestly fraternity, like that of the bishops, this "affectus collegialis" (collegial affection), helps us so much in Italy and throughout the world. It helps everyone, it helps me; it helps the Pope to meet, to share with the bishops of the various countries of the world, of different continents, of different Churches, to share their problems, to talk and be together, to celebrate together, and to eat together too... This last aspect should not be neglected, should not be overlooked. We know that the Lord himself did the same. Even after the Resurrection he came and asked: "Do you have anything to eat?" (cf. Jn 21:5).

51.   Dear women and men religious, Sisters and Brothers, in the Church of Arezzo-Cortona-Sansepolcro, as in all of the Church, you have an important position as consecrated persons — this is a great dignity, a great vocation — and then as Congregations, as communities.

Thank you for the witness of your consecration! You are truly the spiritual "lung" of the Church, the diocese, the parishes. In a special way the contemplative are so, those who by their life of prayer, sacrifice and seclusion obtain countless favors from God and support the work of the priests and the other pastoral workers.

In today's society, threatened by a secularism which confines life to a narrow, worldly perspective, you are asked to bear witness to the Eternal One, to the Absolute of God, the Love which is God, who has revealed himself as Love in Christ Jesus. He so loved the world. All of you, trust in the Lord who has called you and pray insistently for new vocations; I am praying with you (...).

True, the air we breathe today is so often alien to Christian values that it sometimes makes it hard to bear witness, and it could even ask heroic courage of you. But never yield to the temptation to feel abandoned. To you too Jesus says as he said to the apostles: "Do not let your hearts be troubled!" (Jn 14:1). "I am with you!" As I am with the bishops, as I am with the priests, with the consecrated persons, the religious, so too am I with you, my witnesses in the lay vocation; I am with you because I am with the whole apostolic Church. And you have a great part in this apostolate of the apostolic Church, as Vatican II says: the Christian vocation is always a vocation to the apostolate (...).

9

MESSAGE TO THE SUPERIOR GENERAL OF THE CONGREGATION OF THE BLESSED SACRAMENT

June 2, 1993

52.   On the occasion of the conclusion of the thirty-first General Chapter of your Congregation, it is my pleasure to extend to you a very cordial greeting. At this time when you have just been elected Superior General, I offer you my fervent best wishes for the successful fulfillment of your mandate.

I would like to assure the members of the Chapter and your fellow religious, present in each and every continent, that I am close to them in my thoughts and in my prayer before the Blessed Sacrament of our Lord.

The work of Saint Peter Julian Eymard, your Founder, began in humble circumstances but has since developed in a providential way: today you are active in many countries where you find yourselves in very diverse and, at times, very difficult situations. I note that, for the first time, your Chapter has witnessed to the life of the Church throughout the world, and especially in Asia and Africa.

The General Chapter decided, in accordance with your Rule of life, "to promote the unity of the Congregation, to renew it in fidelity to its mission and to formulate a project in response to the needs of the Church and the world" (n. 68). Your reflection took as its starting point the "Mission Project" which had been formulated in the preceding Chapter: "To become prophetic communities, witnesses to the Eucharist, committed, together with the laity, to the building up of Christian communities, whose center of life is the Eucharist, proclamation of the Lord's Passover, power and call for liberation and communion."

53.   In conformity with this orientation, your Chapter sought to renew the life of the Congregation of the Blessed Sacrament under the inspiration of the teaching of Saint Peter Julian Eymard. This man of fire was possessed by Christ's love as revealed to us in his Eucharist; he ardently desired to manifest it to his contemporaries. Along with his companions, he inaugurated a form of religious life in which the Eucharist is the heart. His life, nourished by the Eucharist which he celebrated and contemplated, was enriched with ministries of all kinds. Under the influence of the Holy Spirit, he saw "how much a force for renewal the Eucharist constitutes for the Church and society" (*Rule of life,* n. 33).

Take then as your inspiration the exceedingly rich testimony which your Founder has handed down to you and, in fidelity to his grace, make your inheritance fruitful for the good and the growth of the Church.

Vatican II forcefully reminded us that the Eucharist is primordial for the life of each Christian community: "No Christian community can be built up unless it has its base and its center in the celebration of the Eucharist; it is here, therefore, that all education in the spirit of community must begin. But if a celebration is to be sincere and complete it must lead to various works of charity and mutual help as well as to missionary activity and different forms of Christian witness" (*Presbyterorum ordinis,* n. 6).

54.   Faced with the challenges of our time, your specific contribution to the "new evangelization" should consist in a deeper penetration into the Eucharistic mystery, together with a commitment to proclaim the Gospel to the men and women of this present age,

particularly the poor, in the diversity of their situations and in harmony with the spirit of their particular cultures. This mission presupposes of course that you never cease to deepen your own particular spirituality.

The Eucharist is "the mystery of faith." As Vatican II teaches us: "The Holy Eucharist contains the entire spiritual riches of the Church, that is, Christ himself, who is our Passover, the living bread, whose flesh, vivified by the Holy Spirit and itself vivifying, gives life to men, inviting them and leading them to offer, in union with him, their life, their labors and the whole of creation" (*Presbyterorum ordinis*, n. 5). Therefore, let the celebration of the paschal mystery become more and more the source of your commitment to the service of the Gospel!

55.   It is your aim "to consider the Eucharistic mystery in its totality, in the celebration of Mass as well as in the cult given to the Holy Species conserved after Mass in order to extend the grace of the sacrifice" (*Roman Ritual*, Holy Communion and Eucharistic cult outside the Mass, n. 4). Be faithful to the contemplation of Christ present in the Blessed Sacrament, in order to interiorize what the Church celebrates; know how to introduce the faithful to this special form of prayer through your witness and your ministry.

In imitation of Christ, who gave his life for the world, you should be authentic witnesses to the power for renewal that flows from the Eucharist; let it be celebrated in such a way that it truly becomes for each Christian community a proclamation of the mystery of salvation, our strength in the struggle against sin, a source of reconciliation, pardon and liberation, the primary leaven of unity for the Church and of peace for the world. You should remain committed to the formation of communities nourished by the Eucharist, open to sharing and dedicated to the promotion of human dignity, especially of the poorest of our brothers and sisters.

56.   Your mission at the heart of the Church must resound throughout the world. You should not only *make* the Eucharist but *live* the Eucharist as religious. Be adorers in spirit and in truth! Draw from the celebration of this mystery, and from the prayer that flows from it, the principles of the renewal of your spirituality! Let it also be a source of growth for the laity who are associated with you in your mission!

I ask the Blessed Virgin Mary, Mother of Jesus, who prayed with the Apostles in the Upper Room and who shared the life of the primitive community of Jerusalem, to sustain you in your religious life and apostolate. May the Lord, through the power of his Spirit, renew you in your fidelity to your vocation!

10

TO PRIESTS AND SEMINARIANS IN MADRID

June 16, 1993

57. You have come together on this radiant morning to praise God the Father through Jesus Christ and in the communion and peace of the Spirit for the day that we begin, for having redeemed us by his eternal sacrifice and, most of all, to *thank him for the precious gift of the vocation to the priesthood and consecrated life.*

You have come from every diocese in Spain and from the many formation houses of Institutes of consecrated life and Societies of apostolic life. The places, the circumstances and the concrete ways of realizing your vocation are very different. However, at its deepest root and in its fundamental meaning each of your vocations is identical, because it is born of the love of Jesus Christ for each of you.

"Love never fails" (1 Cor 13:8), we have just heard in the reading of the apostle Paul. From that love that never fails and which exceeds every limit, is born the Church, humanity redeemed by the love of Christ and enabled through the gift of his Holy Spirit to *abide in that love* that is the *fullness of the human vocation.*

58. In meeting you today, dear seminarians from so many places in Spain, great joy fills my Pastor's heart. *The Lord has looked on each of you* with infinite tenderness and love, *to live a story of salvation with you* and to unite you in a special way to his person through the sacrament of Orders. How could I not feel full of joy before this promise of future priests, of generous workers in the harvest with which the Lord blesses us? How can I not rejoice with all of you, with your bishops and

formation personnel, with your respective dioceses and with the whole Church, in seeing the call of Christ bear fruit in your heart?

In this regard, I cannot fail to express my sincere gratitude to so many educators and teachers who, by their work — at times hidden and full of sacrifice — render a valuable service to the Church in such a delicate field as that of the preparation of the future ministers of God.

The hymn to charity that we proclaimed in Lauds places us in the moment of grace that we are living. "Love never fails," says the Apostle; and the *New Covenant in Jesus Christ* is proof of *God's eternal love*, of his infinite goodness towards mankind. In this meeting for prayer I want to help you to penetrate this profound mystery of the covenant so that you may prepare to live it one day with full responsibility and dedication. The Church, aware of the *importance of your formation for the sacred ministry*, reflected during *the last Synod of Bishops* on the formation of priests in present circumstances; I then presented its findings in the Apostolic Exhortation *Pastores dabo vobis*, fully confident that you who are preparing for the priesthood will make it your own.

59.   The secret of your whole formation — human, spiritual, intellectual and pastoral — is to be found in your *configuration to Christ*. In fact, *the priest is "another Christ."* It is only by identifying with him that you will find your own identity, your own joy and your own apostolic fruitfulness. Therefore, the formation that you receive in the seminary must be aimed at preparing you "to enter into communion with the charity of Christ, the Good Shepherd" (*Pastores dabo vobis*, n. 57). The covenant of Christ, his total gift — even giving his life — expresses the *charity of the Good Shepherd* who gives his life in abundance to his sheep. This same charity *must shape*, therefore, *the life of the pastors of the Church*.

In your process of being configured to Christ, the seminary must offer an irreplaceable aid because it is in the formation phase that the foundations of future ministry are laid. Special attention must be given to maturing in the experience of God, which is achieved through *personal and communal prayer and reaches its climax in the Eucharist.* Your experience of prayer during formation will enable you to appraise and evaluate the different ways by which the Lord seeks to communicate with people. Thus, with skill you will be able to guide those who come to you with hearts longing for God. It is for this reason that the seminary must *foster specific times of prayer* and the discernment needed for those forms of prayer which the Church values in particular.

60.   The focal point of the spiritual life of the candidate for the priesthood must be the *daily Eucharist.* In this regard I wish to recall the words of the Apostolic Exhortation *Pastores dabo vobis:* "It is fitting that seminarians take part *every day* in the Eucharistic celebration, in such a way that afterwards they will take up as a rule of their priestly life this daily celebration" (n. 48). By the redeeming mystery of Christ, renewed in the Eucharist, *the sense of mission*, the ardent love for mankind, is nourished. From the Eucharist one also understands that all participation in the priesthood of Christ has a *universal dimension*. It is necessary to educate the heart in this perspective, so that we experience the drama of those peoples and multitudes who still do not know Christ, and so that we may always be ready to go to any part of the world to proclaim him to "all nations" (cf. Mt 28:19). This availability to which I urged you particularly in the Encyclical *Redemptoris missio* — is especially necessary today, before the vast horizons which are open to the mission of the Church and before the challenges of the new evangelization.

61. The *configuration to Christ* must be the main objective of the formation of every candidate for the priesthood. Just as the Lord taught his disciples and prepared them to carry out his mission, so too the Church, following his example, must devote the greatest care to the proper preparation of her priests. "If the Church desires good ministers" said Saint John of Avila, patron of the Spanish clergy, "she must provide for their formation" (*Obras completes*, t. VI, BAC n. 324, Madrid 1971, p. 40). Formation, as the Church intends it, is addressed to the whole person and not only to his intellect. It is meant to make the future priest an authentic "manifestation and image of the Good Shepherd" (*Pastores dabo vobis*, n. 49), so that, in the human, spiritual, intellectual and pastoral fields, he may be a master in the "art of arts" which, according to Saint Gregory the Great, is the care of souls. For this reason the seminary must be a school of priestly formation in its deepest sense.

62. All this emphasizes even more the *importance of study*, aimed not only at acquiring knowledge, but as a complementary part of one's vocation—at a human, spiritual and priestly level — which matures the person in his search for the truth, strengthens him in possessing it and fills him with joy in contemplating it. Without the discipline and the habit of study, the future priest will not be able to be the wise man who, according to the Gospel, in season and out of season exhorts with the Word of God, convinces through truth and frees from error. The priest is called to be a teacher of the Christian faith and he must therefore be able to explain the faith which he preaches and teaches.

Dedication to study must be accomplished in a pastoral perspective because it prepares seminarians for the specific ministries of the pastor: preaching, catechesis and teaching, spiritual counsel and guidance and wise discernment of the will of God in the lives of others. This pastoral dimension of study certainly requires particular attention to the problems of the world today. The priest must be aware of what is happening around him, of the cultural movements of his time, of the currents of thought. Only in this way can the problems which affect man be enlightened with the light of Christian revelation, bringing the truth which comes from Jesus Christ.

63.   The training of seminarians, the Decree of Vatican II *Optatam totius* states, "should have as its object to make them true shepherds of souls after the example of our Lord Jesus Christ, Teacher, Priest and Shepherd" (n. 4). The aim of your whole formation process must be to achieve *full communion with the pastoral charity of Jesus Christ* (cf. *Pastores dabo vobis*, n. 57). This communion will enable you, in the midst of people, to render the Lord Jesus present in all your actions. From this derives the importance of attaining "the same attitude that is also yours in Christ Jesus" (Phil 2:5).

    The priest, who is called to make Christ's redemption present through the sacraments, must always live with the same concern as the Lord: the salvation of man. The priestly ministry would be emptied of content if, in pastoral contact with people, its Christian soteriological dimension were forgotten. This happens, unfortunately, in the reductive forms of exercise of ministry, as if it were a function of mere human, social or psychological support. The priest, like Jesus, is sent to mankind to help people discover their vocation as children of God, to awaken in them — as Jesus did in the Samaritan woman — a yearning for the supernatural life. The priest is sent to move hearts to conversion, educating the moral conscience and reconciling people with God through the sacrament of Penance.

64.   To live fully union with Christ at the service of others, the Lord enriches you with the *gift of celibacy freely assumed* for the sake of the Kingdom, by which the call to the priesthood is sealed. Celibacy configures you to the virginal Christ, Spouse of the Church, to which you are to give yourselves totally in order to render her holy and to make her bear fruit in charity. Celibacy permits you to present yourselves to the Christian people as free men, with the freedom of Christ, to give yourselves unreservedly to universal charity, to spiritual fatherhood, to serve others unconditionally. You will be emotionally mature to the degree to which you welcome *Jesus Christ, poor, chaste and obedient.*

Do not therefore look at what you are giving up, but rather look at what you receive. Do not dwell on renunciation; *look at the gift and contemplate the grace received.* This attitude of living in giving one's life is not improvised nor is it acquired automatically with the sacrament of Orders. It requires special instruction, the development of which involves the whole seminary formation process. In this you will certainly be helped by the experience of wise and holy priests, indispensable spiritual guidance, contact with those among whom you will have your first pastoral experiences and, naturally, the friendships formed with one another and with Christ who calls you to be his friends. This friendship, fostered by community life — which must be carefully cultivated — will help you later to live the priestly fraternity which Vatican II presents as an effective way to make the gift of priesthood even more fruitful (cf. *Presbyterorum ordinis*, n. 8). The experience of this fellowship will be the best preparation for achieving *affective and effective communion in the diocesan presbyterate.*

65.   I cannot conclude this touching meeting without addressing a word of affectionate greeting to the

priests present and, through them, to those throughout Spain.
Dear brothers in the priesthood of Jesus Christ, I want to express my sincere gratitude to you for your dedication, which is silent and not without sacrifice, in the various fields of pastoral activity. Daily stir up the charism which you received through the imposition of hands (cf. 2 Tim 1:6), identifying with Jesus Christ in his threefold office of sanctifying, teaching and nourishing. I entreat you to continue your pastoral work in the service of the People of God with enthusiasm, in intimate communion with your pastors and in keeping with the teaching of the Church.

Love never fails! The call of Christ never fails; it is renewed every day. Try therefore also to renew your encounter with him. May intimate contact with Jesus Christ be an authentic necessity of your lives. One day you had an unforgettable experience of meeting the Lord. That call filled you with joy. That first seed — which was a promise of fullness in love — must grow and bear fruit within you. And so, every instant of your lives will be like that first grace, which is continuously renewed. And, as time goes by, your joy will grow and no one will be able to take it from you, because "love never fails" (1 Cor 13:8).

It only remains for me to encourage you in this journey to reach out to Christ. He reached out to you first. Allow yourselves to be formed by him. Love the Church without reserve; may Mary, the Mother of Christ the Priest, educate you with her motherly love, so that the authentic image of her Son may be reflected in you.

11

LETTER TO THE POOR CLARES ON THE OCCASION OF THE EIGHTH CENTENARY OF THE BIRTH OF SAINT CLARE

August 11, 1993

66.　　Eight hundred years ago, Clare of Assisi was born to the nobleman, Favarone di Offreduccio. This "new woman," as the Ministers General of the Franciscan families wrote of her in a recent letter, lived as a "little plant" in the shadow of Saint Francis, who led her to the heights of Christian perfection. The celebration of such a truly evangelical creature is meant most of all to be an invitation to rediscover contemplation, that spiritual journey which only the mystics experience deeply. To read her ancient biography and her writings — the *Form of Life,* her *Testament,* and the *four extant Letters* of the many she wrote to Saint Agnes of Prague — means being so immersed in the mystery of the triune God and of Christ, the incarnate Word, as to be dazzled. Her writings are so marked by the love stirred up in her by her ardent, prolonged gazing upon Christ the Lord that it is not easy to express what only a woman's heart could experience.

67.　　Clare's contemplative journey, which will culminate in her vision of the "King of glory" (*Proc* IV, 19), begins precisely in her total abandonment to the Spirit of the Lord, after the example of Mary at the Annunciation: that is to say, it begins with that spirit of poverty (cf. Lk 1:48) which empties her of everything but the simplicity of a gaze fixed on God.

　　For Clare, poverty — which she loved so much and mentioned so often in her writings — is the wealth of the soul which, stripped of its own goods, is open to the "Spirit of the Lord and his holy manner of working" (cf. RC1 X, 10), like an empty vessel in which God can pour out an abundance of his gifts. The parallel between Mary and Clare appears in Saint Francis' earliest writing, in the *Forma vivendi* he gave to Clare: "By divine inspiration you have made yourselves daughters and servants of the Most High King, the heavenly Father, and have taken the Holy Spirit as your spouse, choosing to live according to the perfection of the holy Gospel" (*Forma vivendi*, in RC1 VI, 3).

Clare and her sisters are called "spouses of the Holy Spirit": an expression not common in the Church's history, in which a sister, a nun, is always described as the "spouse of Christ." However, here we have the resonance of some expressions from Luke's account of the Annunciation (cf. Lk 1:26-38), which become key words for expressing Clare's experience: *the Most High, the Holy Spirit, the Son of God, the handmaid of the Lord* and, lastly, that "overshadowing" which for Clare is her investiture, when her hair was shorn and fell at the foot of our Lady's altar in the Portiuncula, "before her bridal chamber, as it were" (cf. *Leg*C1 8).

68.   The Spirit of the Lord and his holy manner of working," which is given to us in baptism, is that of creating in a Christian the image of the Son of God. In solitude and silence, which Clare chooses as a form of life for herself and her sisters within the most poor walls of her monastery halfway between Assisi and the Portiuncula, the curtain of smoke of words and earthly things fades away, and communion with God becomes a reality: love which is born and which gives of itself.

Clare, bowed down in contemplating the Infant of Bethlehem, exhorts us: Since this vision "is the splendor of eternal glory, the brilliance of eternal light and the mirror without blemish, gaze upon that mirror each day.... Look at the poverty of him who was placed in a manger and wrapped in swaddling clothes. O marvelous humility! O astonishing poverty! The King of angels, the Lord of heaven and earth, is laid in a manger" (4LAg 14, 19-21).

69.   She did not even notice that through her contemplation and transformation, her womb as a consecrated and "poor virgin" attached to the "poor Christ" (cf. 2LAg 18) had become a cradle of the Son of God (*Proc* IX, 4). It is the voice of this Child which, at a time of great danger — when the monastery was about to fall into the hands of Saracen troops in the employ of Emperor Frederick II — reassures her from the Eucharist: "I will always protect you!" (*Leg*C1 22).

On Christmas eve in 1252, the Child Jesus bore Clare far away from her bed of illness and love, which knows neither time nor place, and enveloped her in a mystical experience which immersed her in the infinite abyss of God.

70.   If Catherine of Siena is the Saint full of passion for the Blood of Christ, if the great Saint Teresa is the woman who goes from "mansion" to "mansion" to the threshold of the great King in the Interior Castle, and if Thérèse of the Child Jesus is the one who, in Gospel simplicity, travels the little way, Clare is the *passionate lover of the poor, crucified Christ,* with whom she wants to identify absolutely.

She puts it thus in one of her letters: "Look upon him who became contemptible for you, and follow him, making yourself contemptible in this world for him. Your Spouse, though more beautiful than the children of men, became for your salvation the lowest of men, was despised, struck, scourged untold times throughout his entire body, and then died amid the suffering of the cross.... Gaze upon him, meditate upon him, contemplate him, as you desire to imitate him. If you suffer with him, you shall rejoice with him; if you die with him on the cross of tribulation, you shall possess heavenly mansions in the splendor of the saints, and in the Book of Life your name shall be called glorious among men" (2LAg 19-22).

71.   Clare, who entered the monastery when she was but eighteen years of age, died there at the age of fifty-nine, after a life of suffering, of constant prayer, strict observance and penance. Because of this "ardent desire for the poor, crucified Christ," nothing burdened her, to the point that at the end of her life she could say to Brother Raynaldo, who assisted her "in the long martyrdom of so many illnesses," that: "After I once came to know the grace of my Lord Jesus Christ through his servant Francis, no pain has been bothersome, no penance too severe, no weakness, dearly beloved brother, has been hard" (LegC1 44).
        But the One who suffers on the cross is he who reflects the Father's glory and sweeps away in his Passover those who loved him to the point of sharing his suffering out of love for him.

72.   The delicate eighteen year-old who, fleeing home on the night of Palm Sunday 1212, set off without hesitation on the adventure of a new experience, believing in the Gospel as Francis showed her, and in nothing else, with the eyes of her body and of her heart totally immersed in the poor and crucified Christ, experiences this union which transforms her: "Place your mind before the mirror of eternity," she writes to Agnes of Prague. "Place your soul in the brilliance of glory! Place your heart in the figure of the divine substance! And transform your entire being into the image of the Godhead itself through contemplation, so that you too may feel what his friends feel as they taste the hidden sweetness that God himself has reserved from the

beginning for those who love him. Since you have cast aside all (those) things which, in this deceitful and turbulent world, ensnare their blind lovers, love him totally who gave himself totally for your love" (3LAg 12-15).

73.　Thus the hard bed of the cross becomes the sweet nuptial bed and the "life-long recluse of love" finds the most passionate accents of the beloved in the Song of Songs: "Draw me after you, ... O heavenly Spouse! I will run and not tire, until you bring me into the wine-cellar" (4LAg 30-31).

Enclosed in the monastery of San Damiano, in a life marked by poverty, hard work, tribulation and illness, as well as a fraternal communion so intense that, in the language of the "Form of Life," it could be described as "holy unity" (RC1, *Bull of Innocent IV*, 2), Clare experiences the purest joy experienced by any creature: the joy of living in Christ the perfect union of the three divine Persons, entering as it were into the ineffable circuit of Trinitarian love.

74.　Clare's life, under the guidance of Francis, was not an eremitic life, even though it was contemplative and cloistered. Around her, wanting to live like the birds of the air and the lilies of the field (Mt 6:26, 28), gathered the first group of sisters, for whom God alone sufficed. This "little flock," which rapidly expanded — by August 1228 there were at least twenty-five monasteries of "Poor Clares" (cf. Letter of Cardinal Raynaldo: *Archivium Franciscanum Historicum* 5, 1912, pp. 444-446) — had no fear (cf. Lk 12:32). The faith was the reason for their peaceful security in the face of every danger. Clare and her sisters had hearts as big as the world: as contemplatives, they interceded for the whole of humanity. Those souls who were sensitive to the daily problems of each person were able to take all difficulties upon themselves; there was no concern, suffering, anguish or discouragement of others which did not find an echo in the hearts of these prayerful women. Clare cried and pleaded with the Lord for her beloved city of Assisi when it was under siege by the troops of Vitale of Aversa, obtaining the city's liberation from war; every day she prayed for the sick and often healed them with a sign of the cross. Convinced that there can be no apostolic life unless it is immersed in the open side of Christ crucified, she wrote to Agnes of Prague in the words of Saint Paul: "I consider you a coworker of God himself (cf. Rom 16:3) and a support of the weak members of his ineffable Body" (3LAg8).

75.   Due to a type of iconography which has been very popular since the seventeenth century, Clare is often depicted holding a monstrance. This gesture recalls, although in a more solemn posture, the humble reality of this woman who, although she was very sick, prostrated herself with the help of two sisters before the silver ciborium containing the Eucharist (cf. LegC1 21), which she had placed in front of the refectory door that the Emperor's troops were about to storm. Clare lived on that pure Bread which, according to the custom of the time, she could receive only seven times a year. On her sickbed she embroidered corporals and sent them to the poor churches in the Spoleto valley.

76.   In reality Clare's whole life was a *eucharist* because, like Francis, from her cloister she raised up a continual "thanksgiving" to God in her prayer, praise, supplication, intercession, weeping, offering and sacrifice. She accepted everything and offered it to the Father in union with the infinite "thanks" of the only-begotten Son, the Child, the Crucified, the risen One, who lives at the right hand of the Father. (...)

12

TO PRIESTS, RELIGIOUS AND SEMINARIANS IN VILNIUS, LITHUANIA

September 4, 1993

77. I thank the Lord for the gift of this meeting, to which I have particularly looked forward. I greet each of you with joy, as I do all the priests and the men and women religious who could not be here because of age or illness. I am also aware of the spiritual closeness of those who have died, and who, from heaven, still accompany the journey of the Church for which they gave their energies, and on occasion, their lives.

I am particularly pleased that our first meeting takes place in the cathedral of Vilnius, which was closed in 1950 and reopened for worship in 1989. In this church, where the heart of the Lithuanian nation beats, are proudly preserved the mortal remains of Saint Casimir, which were returned to the chapel dedicated to him on March 4, 1989. I have just now paused before them in prayer, in gratitude to your patron for my being allowed the joy to be among you.

In this family atmosphere, how can I fail to remember the many bishops and priests who devoted their lives to the Gospel with heroic fidelity? Above all, Blessed George Matulaitis, the Ordinary of Vilnius from 1918 to 1925, whom I had the honor of raising to the glory of the altars in 1987. And Archbishop Julijonas Steponavicius, who was impeded in his mission from 1961 to 1988, when he was able once more to take up the pastoral care of the archdiocese. At his death in 1991 he was buried in this cathedral. I also recall Archbishop Mecislovas Reinys, who was appointed coadjutor of

Vilnius in 1940, arrested in 1947, and died as a martyr in 1953 in the prison of Vladimir, in Russia.

Their witness is a source of encouragement and support for the Church in Lithuania along the way which lies ahead.

78.   Dear brothers and sisters, you have emerged from a long period in which the faith was cruelly tested, like precious metal in a crucible. *But the hour of forced silence about God is now being followed by the time of the courageous proclamation of the Gospel* and the building of the Kingdom through your personal witness. Suffering and the Cross will never disappear: *yesterday's trials will certainly be followed by new ones today and tomorrow.* The strenuous task of evangelization will be carried out in different ways, but it will always be an expression of the one Cross of Christ, that Cross which rises above your churches and which must reign in the hearts of all who believe. You yourselves will have to face misunderstanding on the part of those who, as the result of an atheistic education, may have lost — at least temporarily — their appreciation of religion. You will have to deal with indifference, misunderstanding, tendencies towards secularization, and psychological isolation within a society which is undergoing profound transformations. You will have to respond, in particular, to the disturbing phenomenon of the sects, whose proliferation is abetted by widespread misconceptions about religion.

79.   After having celebrated the sixth centenary of its baptism a few years ago, Lithuania is now experiencing a delicate moment in its long and noble history. Once known as "the land of the crosses" because its fields and roads were filled with them, Lithuania has unfortunately become a way of the cross for so many of its children.

Now, at the dawn of a time of renewed hope, it is important that *the priest in particular, be looked upon by his fellow countrymen as a brother of the Redeemer,* who died on the Cross and rose again. Conformed to the Crucified Christ, the priest is called to be *a man of forgiveness and reconciliation.*

80.   Dear priests, you must be Good Samaritans to your brothers and sisters who carry the weight of a past dominated by suspicion and fear of informers, of long years of silence about God and even of deceitful attempts to deny God. You are being asked to help rebuild the social and human fabric of your country, with patience, love and persevering apostolic fervor.

In your eyes, there must be neither winners nor losers, but rather men and women who need to be helped to leave error behind; persons to be supported in their efforts to recover from the effects, including the psychological ones, of violence, abuse of power, and the violation of human rights. You need to remind the "losers" that it is not enough to adapt to changed social situations: instead what is required is sincere conversion and, if necessary, expiation. And the "winners" need to hear continually the exhortation to *forgiveness,* so that there will come about that authentic peace which derives from following the Gospel of mercy and of charity.

Now then is the time to appreciate more fully the theological roots of your priestly ministry. In order that the world may believe, *priests must more than ever be "men of the Trinity."*

81.   *The priest, as a son of the heavenly Father,* is called to *reflect God's fatherhood in his everyday life.* It is not by chance that the very title which you are often given by the "sensus fidelium" is that of "Father."

As sons of the Father "who is seated on high, who looks far down upon the heavens and the earth" (Ps

113:5-6), *you must be in the forefront of those who serve their brethren,* experiencing with them the problems and the difficulties of this Lithuania which is being reborn. Make your own the mind of Christ, our Master and Savior, who came "not to be served but to serve" (Mk 10:45). Give witness of your detachment and generosity. The evangelical poverty which the Lord demands of all who wish to follow him closely (cf. Mt 19:29) *is a wellspring of apostolic fruitfulness and of personal happiness.* Be generous, and may your open-heartedness be a source and stimulus to the growth of a fraternal spirit.

Deeply rooted in the fatherhood of God, you must proclaim to the world *that only love,* the love which the Holy Spirit pours out in the hearts of believers (cf. Rom 5:5), *can offer solid foundations for building the earthly city,* for it gives meaning and fruitfulness even to sacrifices and trials.

82.   Like the Good Shepherd, welcome and seek out every person. All people, but particularly the young, are looking for "spiritual fathers," enlightened guides, teachers of evangelical consistency. *Listen, encourage, support and lead* God's People along the paths of truth and holiness: *this is your mission,* and it obviously requires of you a constant effort to be faithful and to love Christ, the Redeemer of man. Set always before yourselves the example of Jesus; carry on a daily conversation with the divine Master, a conversation of openness to his word and readiness to follow. In this way you will become *instruments of the Holy Spirit* whom he has sent.

The Extraordinary Synod held twenty years after the close of the Second Vatican Council had this to say: "Because the Church in Christ is a mystery, she must be considered a sign and instrument of holiness. For this reason the Council proclaimed the vocation of all the faithful to holiness (cf. *Lumen gentium,* chap. 5). The call to holiness is an invitation to an intimate conversion of heart and to participation in the life of God, One and Triune... Men and women saints have always been sources of renewal in difficult circumstances throughout the Church's history. Today we have tremendous need of saints, for whom we must assiduously implore God" (Synod of Bishops, *Final Relatio* of the Extraordinary Assembly on the Twentieth Anniversary of the Close of the Second Vatican Council, II, A, 4).

83.   Dear priests, your ministry is a gift of God which is meant to build up the holiness of his people. How can you train others in Christian perfection if you yourselves are not the first to be led by the Holy Spirit? Ask the Holy Spirit, with humility and perseverance, for the grace of holiness. And encourage others to ask for that gift, especially those who are most sensitive and those who suffer, those who, like Simon the Cyrenian, help Christ in carrying his Cross.

The holiness demanded of the priest is not an external holiness, limited to the sacredness of the actions of his ministry. It consists in a progressive *identification with Christ* and the will of the Father in his providential plan. The holy priest is the one who does God's will with docility. It makes little difference when or where. Identification with Christ is to be sought in the parishes of the cities and in those of the country. In all times and places the priest is called to empty himself, in order to be filled all the more with God.

84.   The People of God, impelled by the one Spirit of Christ, are able to perceive *in the spiritual fatherhood* of the priest the most *profound reason for the celibacy* which the Latin Church requires of her ministers. With the eyes of faith, Christians are able to see in the consecration to virginity of those called to the priestly ministry and the religious life *a flame capable of giving*

warmth and light to the world. Celibacy is thus not a renunciation; in its own way it is essentially an affirmation of spousal love which, as such, requires total giving. And precisely from such a free and generous love there will spring up a renewed spiritual vigor for your apostolic ministry.

85.   Dear priests! At this moment of history, the demands of the pastoral ministry require that *you pay heed to the social concerns of your people.*
        The Lord asks you today, as he did the Twelve (Mt 14:16), to help him to "feed the crowd," by distributing loaves and fish; at times these may be tragically scarce, yet he is capable of making them abound. Work then to deepen your knowledge of the *Church's social doctrine,* which can provide the faithful with important facts and encouragement for resolving the more urgent questions now facing your country after so long a period of forced social silence. The Church does not claim to offer concrete solutions to social problems. But her doctrine does contain valuable principles and useful criteria which can inspire general policies and specific decisions. The Church offers Lithuania a rich heritage of values ultimately inspired by the proclamation of salvation contained in the Word of God and revealed in Jesus Christ.

86.   It can happen however that precisely from this desire to serve man in his social as well as his private dimension, there can arise situations of tension or suspicion between the Church and representatives of political power. You, the priests of Lithuania, have known this from bitter experience in the recent past. During the period of occupation it was forbidden to preach the Gospel and to engage in social work on behalf of the poor. With the return to democracy, it is to be hoped that relations between Church and State

will develop according to criteria of mutual respect, resisting the temptations either of secularism or of clericalism. The State in fact must not intrude upon the autonomy which the Constitution and international Conventions recognize as rightfully belonging to religion, nor must priests, in the exercise of their mission of evangelization, intervene in party politics or in the direct governance of the nation. Like so many other States in Europe and in the world, your country, too, will be able to draw great advantages from a frank dialogue between Church and State, provided that on the one hand the legitimate representatives of the Lithuanian people take care to respect the freedom of the ecclesial community, and the Church's ministers, on the other, refrain from any kind of undue interference in the sphere proper to civic institutions.

87.   Here I also wish to emphasize another aspect of your role as pastors of souls in Lithuania. It is the need to *acquire and strengthen the so-called human virtues* which the priest must cultivate above all in his own life, so as then to teach them to the people entrusted to his care.

After every significant social upheaval, man bears scars both in his patterns of behavior and in his soul. In moments such as these, it is more important than ever that consecrated persons give vivid testimony of the close interdependence between the theological and the human virtues. It is from the combination of these that a new humanity, reconciled with itself, will arise. Loyalty, honesty, industriousness, order, trust in others, a spirit of service, cordiality, respect, detachment, generosity, a sense of justice and responsibility, balance, serenity, sincerity: these are some of the characteristic traits of the "new man."

Dear brothers, cultivate these and other similar virtues in your ascetical life and your efforts to follow the way of holiness. *Practicing them is the first contribution to the promotion of the new man* which your homeland needs in order to advance towards the goals of prosperity and peace.

88.   Dear women religious, I now wish to address a special thought to you, together with my profound gratitude for your activity during the difficult years of the recent past. I know of your hidden life, your silent sacrifice, your suffering. How much you have suffered! And with what fidelity you have continued in your mission! During times of harsh oppression you were truly "the salt of the earth," which encouraged and sustained your fellow Christians, keeping alive their faith, hope and charity.

Dear Sisters, the Pope understands your present difficulties and he prays that you will always have the energy and the vigor to renew yourselves, adapting your style of life and apostolate to changed situations in the Church and in society. The Second Vatican Council reminded us that consecrated life is a great gift for the mission of the Church in the world. At the present time, what is demanded of Institutes dedicated to the various works of the apostolate is authentic holiness, effective communal sharing, apostolic activity and the witness of charity (cf. *Perfectae caritatis*, n. 8). May the Lord guide you in this time of profound social change, pointing out to each religious family the way to proceed in order best to respond to God's plan.

89.   Today there is need for consecrated persons who, through prayer, sacrifice and their specific activities, can contribute effectively to the much-desired spiritual rebirth of Lithuania. For this reason, it is indispensable that aspirants to religious life receive a training which corresponds to present-day circum-

stances; fortunately these are quite different from those of the totalitarian regime of the past.

Finally a few words to you, dear candidates for the priesthood. You too have need of a solid and enlightened formation, sustained by a constant seeking for God. The same holiness needed by priests is demanded of you, together with a similar availability and generosity. *Brightly-burning lamps of charity and holiness:* this is what your lives are called to become.

90.   Look to Mary, dwelling-place of the Trinity, who is venerated here in Lithuania with particular devotion in the shrines of Ausros Vartai and of Siluva, to which I will go on pilgrimage! Look to her, priests and aspirants to the priestly life, men and women religious and all those whom God calls to work in his vineyard.

Daughter of the Father and Mother of Christ, Mary is Mother of the Church and Queen of the Apostles. On Calvary, Christ himself gave her as a Mother to all of us, in the person of John. The Apostles were gathered in prayer with Mary when the Holy Spirit descended upon them on the day of Pentecost. To Mary I entrust all of you, that your service of love will produce abundant fruits of evangelical life. The Church and your homeland will benefit greatly from them.

May my apostolic blessing bring you comfort and support.

13

TO THE MONASTIC COMMUNITY
OF CAMALDOLI, ITALY

September 17, 1993

91.   I am grateful to the Lord who has given me the
opportunity to visit the Franciscan shrine of La
Verna this morning, and to meet you, the Monks of
Camaldoli, in this splendid hermitage of yours, founded
by *Saint Romuald* at the dawn of the second millennium.
Between *La Verna* and *Camaldoli* there are deep historical and spiritual bonds. Indeed, among your cells there
is one where Francis of Assisi lived for a while.

Dear brothers and sisters, I greet you all with
affection. I thank the Prior General, Dom Emanuele
Bargellini, for the invitation he addressed to me, and I
am grateful to all of you for having welcomed me with
the hospitality that has always distinguished this religious family. I greet the Camaldolese Nuns, as well as the
Benedictine Oblates present here as a visible witness to
the deep links which unite all those who are inspired by
the Benedictine Rule.

In less than three weeks your Congregation will
be opening its General Chapter, the basic theme of
which is both thought-provoking and demanding: *"Choosing hope, choosing the future."*

Choosing hope and the future implies, in the last
analysis, *choosing God,* the future of history and the
universe, eternally present to him and guided by his
Providence. It means *choosing Christ,* the hope of every
human being.

How is it possible not to think, at this time of
spiritual exchange, of your life's supportive structure, in
other words, that *community liturgical prayer* of which

Benedict states in the Rule: "Nihil operi Dei praeponatur" (Chap. XX — to prefer nothing to the work of God)? Many claim that in Camaldoli the complicated balance between the variety of sacred texts and melodies and the sober tone of the liturgical rite is maintained.

92.   Continue, dear brothers and sisters, in this *service of praise*, certain that it is also the first charitable deed you perform for all those whom Providence, in his mysterious ways, leads here to pray with you. Conversion, as you know by experience, is far more frequently brought about by the Word of God in prayer than by so many human words.

Choosing God also means daily contemplation and meditation on his Word, which is what you do in accordance with your precious monastic tradition, cultivating the *"lectio divina"* which today, through a gift of Divine Wisdom, is shared abundantly with the whole People of God. Pastors are well aware how much the ecclesial community owes to you monks!

Choosing God also means humbly and patiently cultivating, according to God's design, *ecumenical and interreligious dialogue*. Your Order's communities, especially those which have developed in California and India, have been committed for years to this spiritual search, interwoven with prayer and respectful dialogue with Buddhist and Hindu monks. In your monastery too, fruitful Jewish-Christian meetings often take place, on the basis of friendship and mutual esteem, progressive knowledge and cordial mutual acceptance.

"Nihil amori Christi praeponere," (Prefer nothing to the love of Christ), we read again in Benedict's Rule (Chap. IV). Here then, dearly beloved, is another aspect of your mission in the Church: that of cenobitic life and hospitality, openness to Christ who manifests himself in every brother and sister, but especially in the lowliest, the weakest and the most troubled.

In this regard, I am pleased to emphasize the unique *ecclesial dimension of the monk's life,* a dimension which is not lacking even when, through a special divine vocation, he is living in greater solitude or what is known as "reclusion."

The doctrine of the Fathers is well expressed in a passage of the work *"Dominus vobiscum"* by Saint Peter Damian, addressed to the hermit, Leo of Fonte Avellana, who lived "amore supernae libertatis inclusus" ("cloistered for love of eternal freedom"). The holy Doctor wrote: "If we are all one in Christ, each of us possesses in him all that belongs to him and therefore, when through physical solitude we may seem far from the Church, we are always very present within her through the inviolable mystery of unity" (Chap. 10; PL 145, 239 B).

Dear brothers and sisters, choosing hope and the future means *choosing the Spirit of God in Christ.* This particularly occurs in that form of life which God himself brought about in the Church, inspiring *Saint Romuald* to found the Benedictine family of Camaldoli, with its characteristic complementarity of hermitage and monastery, solitary life and cenobitic life in harmony with each other.

93.   Therefore make the most of your next General Chapter, as a time for an important deepening of this *original charism,* passed on to you through a multifaceted, one thousand year-old tradition that has sought to preserve in unity the diverse aspects of your Founder's exceptional intuition. You will thus be able to make Camaldolese monastic life even more transparent and meaningful, in the present-day context of the Church and in the recent international dimension of the Congregation.

And you, dear *Nuns, Daughters of Saint Romuald,* whom I greet and thank for the precious service you render to the Church; continue to offer the Congregation your particular contribution of ascetic commitment, reflection and human and spiritual experience.

Finally, the presence of *Benedictine Oblates* at our short, but intense, meeting is an indication that the monastic experience continues to inspire the progress in faith of many lay people in the Church's life in the world. While I cordially greet the numerous participants at the encounter, I urge them, as lay people, to be witnesses of that primacy of God and Christ which the monks are trying to reflect by their life in the hermitage and in the monastery.

With these sentiments I wholeheartedly impart my apostolic blessing to each of you and to the entire Congregation. I entrust you to Mary, Mother of Christ and of the Church, who faithfully and silently treasured God's Word in her heart.

May you continue on your way with renewed vigor!

14

TO CAPUCHIN FRIARS AT CASTEL GANDOLFO

September 23, 1993

94.   I am very happy to welcome you on the occasion of this Convention on the "Vocations Apostolate and the Postulancy," which concludes a cycle of four international conventions on the different formative stages of religious life according to the Franciscan and Capuchin charism. (...)

The work which you are carrying out in these days is the sign of the Capuchin Order's constant concern for the delicate and fundamental mission of caring for the vocations and formation of the friars.

You form a significant group of brothers, the majority of whom are young, involved in the vocations apostolate and coming from fifty nations on different continents to represent all the Conferences of the Order. You have gathered in Rome to reflect and draw up guidelines on the theme of the prenovitiate. I wish to express to you my sincere satisfaction that you desire to reflect on this primary, fundamental phase of formation, aimed at laying the groundwork for a conscious, serene entrance into the novitiate and for the continuing perseverance of the candidates.

You know how important the pastoral care of vocations to the ordained ministries and to the different forms of consecrated life is today. As I have already had occasion to note in the past, this in fact is "the fundamental problem of the Church" (*Homily,* May 10, 1981; *Insegnamenti,* IV/1, 1149).

95.   As regards the postulancy, I wish to recall on this occasion the directive contained in the Code of

Canon Law: for admission to an Institute of consecrated life "a suitable preparation" (can. 597, §2) is required. In connection with this it should be remembered how the Instructions *"Renovationis causam,"* I, 4 and *"Potissimum institutioni"* n. 42 observe that the greatest difficulties met nowadays in the formation of new novices derive from their insufficient maturity at the time of their entrance into the novitiate.

This present convention offers the opportunity to emphasize some basic criteria, which spring from your special charism and which must lead to timely practical directives for your work at the service of the whole Order.

I urge you, dear brothers, to safeguard the central value of fraternal Gospel living and to devote attention to the quality rather than the number of candidates. May you yourselves be a living vocational model! Keep yourselves in a state of ongoing formation and renewal, so that your whole life and your institutions may witness to the greatness of your mission in the Church.

Do not be afraid to involve your best members in formation and above all in the necessary preparation of the formation teams. For this you must promote fraternal cooperation between those responsible in the different Provinces. It is necessary to renew programs, formation plans and practical options, to make them ever more faithful to your spirituality. In fact it is only in this way that your service to the Church and to society today will contribute to the work of the new evangelization. The Lord will not fail to grant new vocations to your brotherhood.

96.   Dear brothers, I still carry in my heart the recent experience of La Verna which was truly thought-provoking and touching. This vivid memory leads me spontaneously to urge you to love and live deeply the insights and demands of your Franciscan charism. New

generations will follow you, and your formative efforts will be effective to the extent that your example shines like that of Francis. "Centuries pass, and the Saint of Assisi speaks to us as if he were alive today.... With total clarity Saint Francis offers the image of an authentic person, of a successful person ... and he continues to exercise an incredible attraction" that of one whose "voice was so frail yet forceful with the power of the Gospel ... the world longs for" (*Angelus,* September 17, 1993).

While entrusting your journey in fidelity to the Franciscan vocation to Mary, Mother, Teacher and Model of all consecrated life, to each of you I impart my apostolic blessing, and I willingly extend it to the young people on their vocational journey and to your brotherhood spread over the five continents.

15

TO THE GENERAL CHAPTER OF THE SISTERS OF THE HOLY FAMILY OF BORDEAUX

October 30, 1993

97.   At the end of your General Chapter, I am glad to welcome you, representatives of the Sisters of the Holy Family of Bordeaux, present in many countries throughout the world. I greet in particular Sister Joy Smith who has just been elected Superior General, as well as the members of the Council, and I assure them of my good wishes and prayers in the fulfillment of their duties.

These past few days, you have been celebrating the two hundredth anniversary of the death of the Venerable Pierre-Bienvenu Noailles, your founder. I share your joy and your gratitude because the spiritual and apostolic insights of this Servant of God have not ceased to bear abundant fruit in the various branches that constitute what he himself called the Association of the Holy Family.

98.   You have retained your founder's vigorous spirituality connected with his own spiritual experience, which he was well able to pass on. From his seminary days, he was vowed to "God alone"; and he expressed his prayer thus: "You alone are the way and happiness. Surround me with yourself. May I see only you... May I live only for you" (*Notes from Issy*, 1817). He discovered in God "this way of the heart which is an immense love" (*ibid.*), which allowed him to glimpse the richness of the Trinitarian mystery, reflected in the Holy Family of Nazareth, then in the Church.

The deep inner life of the members of the Holy Family was to be the true reference point of Father Noailles' foundations. In "the spirit of God alone," in imitation of the virtues of Jesus, Mary and Joseph, today as in the past, you find the real source of your consecration to the service of God and your apostolate. The 1844 Rule already stated: "The Sisters of the Holy Family (...) will be like the Apostles, consumed by the desire to make our Lord loved and to spread his Kingdom everywhere." The intense work that you have carried out over these past years in connection with the Holy See confirms your fidelity to the founding charism of your Institute and, I am convinced, will help it to flourish.

99.   This meeting gives me the opportunity to express to you the Church's gratitude for all that you contribute by taking your part in her mission of evangelization. I know that your communities are working on the five continents, and particularly in those regions stricken by poverty and by conflicts that are difficult to resolve. In these conditions, your witness and your active devotion are all the more important. As daughters of the Holy Family, you are the valuable artisans of peace and reconciliation.

Today I wish to tell you of the Church's confidence in you, and I encourage you to be united especially through love of God, in order to pursue your ecclesial apostolate. For this reason, watch over the quality of the formation you give to the young women who join you, opening them to an intense spiritual life in the communion of the Church, that they may acquire missionary zeal, so vital in regard to the expectations of the men and women of our time.

100.   Remembering that your founder asks you to continue the invocation "to God alone" in the

motto "All through Mary," I particularly entrust the Sisters of the Holy Family in the apostolic or the contemplative life to the Mother of the Lord. May she always go before you in your pilgrimage of faith and in the works you conduct! May she awaken and sustain vocations, necessary for the vitality of your Institute and for its ecclesial service!

I wholeheartedly impart to you my apostolic blessing which I extend to all your sisters and to all those who are associated with you.

16

TO AN INTERNATIONAL CONGRESS
ORGANIZED BY
THE UNION OF SUPERIORS GENERAL

November 26, 1993

101. Dear Brothers and Sisters, I greet you with joy on the occasion of the International Congress sponsored by the Union of Superiors General.

Your Congress is characterized by its global dimension and by its broad vision, which come from its preparation by the highest authorities of the various religious Institutes. There you were certainly able to experience an intense atmosphere of preparation for the Ordinary Synod of Bishops to be held next year. I hope that the work may provide useful documentation for the Synod meeting.

On the threshold of the third millennium of the Christian era, religious life today is experiencing a particularly significant moment in its history because of the demanding, extensive renewal which has been made necessary by changing social and cultural conditions.

102. The next Ordinary Assembly of the Synod will certainly bring the members of the Church — pastors, clergy, consecrated persons and faithful — to an awareness of this unique moment, so as not to miss the opportunity for a true return to Gospel sources. Indeed, it is Jesus Christ who is the supreme reference point for all religious and for the entire People of God. We should look to him as the unparalleled example of a consecrated person, who, sent into the world, calls his disciples to follow him through the radical gift of self to the heavenly Father and to the faithful.

In the synagogue of Nazareth, as the Evangelist Luke tells us (cf. Lk 4:16-19), Jesus applies Isaiah's messianic prophecy to himself: "The Spirit of the Lord God is upon me..." (Is 61:1). In it he is indicated as "the Consecrated One" par excellence, God's Anointed, the "Christ." This implies a unique presence within him of the Holy Spirit, who unites his mission with his consecration in an indissoluble bond. As I recalled in the Apostolic Exhortation *Pastores dabo vobis,* "the Spirit is not simply 'upon' the Messiah, but he 'fills' him, penetrating every part of him and reaching to the very depths of all that he is and does. Indeed, the Spirit is the principle of the 'consecration' and 'mission' of the Messiah" (n. 19).

In this light, the religious belongs radically to God, and in the Spirit draws on the very sources of holiness and total apostolic giving.

103.   Every consecration in the Church is intrinsically linked to a radical and vital synthesis of consecration and mission. This is expressed through the practice of the evangelical counsels in order to witness to the *Gospel of the beatitudes* among the People of God (cf. *Lumen gentium,* n. 31). This implies a life-style which, accompanied by renunciation and sacrifice, involves an exacting commitment and requires constant and appropriate asceticism.

However, the true reason for this choice does not really consist in planning a life of mortification, but rather in the total option for Jesus Christ. The personal and fascinating discovery of the ineffable mystery of Jesus Christ, crucified and risen, allows us to benefit fully from the cross. Apostolic faith shows us in the Incarnate Word, the true Redeemer of mankind, the "Consecrated One" by antonomasia. Jesus, the Christ, is the measure of all; he indicates life's true purpose to man, and provides him with help to achieve it. In him, the new Adam, the whole of human reality comes to be illuminated with an eschatological meaning, opening wide its horizons beyond time.

104. Thus we can repeat with Saint Paul: "For to me life is Christ..." (Phil 1:21); "yet I live, no longer I, but Christ lives in me" (Gal 2:20); "so whoever is in Christ is a new creation" (2 Cor 5:17). In other words, with the apostle Paul we are convinced that God has proposed, in the plan to be carried out in the fullness of time, "to sum up all things in Christ, in heaven and on earth" (Eph 1:10).

This all-embracing vision of faith offers us the real reason for the radical nature of consecrated life and endows it with fascination and joy. If Jesus Christ is truly the center of life and history, it is worth following him faithfully, participating in the fascinating mystery of his Redemption even when this involves hardship and deprivation.

Dear brothers and sisters, numerous perspectives on renewal stem from these reflections on Christ's mystery. I would like here to pick out a few briefly, which could usefully serve as guidelines in the preparation for the next Synod.

105. Jesus Christ is the supreme reference point for every believer, but in particular for those who are called to give an "outstanding and striking testimony that the world cannot be transfigured and offered to God without the spirit of the beatitudes" (*Lumen gentium*, n. 31).

"Religious should carefully consider," the Council urges, "that through them, to believers and nonbelievers alike, the Church truly wishes to give an increasingly clearer revelation of Christ. Through them Christ should be shown contemplating on the mountain, announcing God's Kingdom to the multitude, healing the sick and the maimed, turning sinners to wholesome fruit, blessing children, doing good to all, and always obeying the will of the Father who sent him" (*Lumen gentium*, n. 46).

Renewal should therefore lead to this in its fullness, and without delay. Indeed, the Church does not need religious who are dazzled by secularism and the appeals of the contemporary world, but courageous witnesses and tireless apostles of the Kingdom.

106. The first basic value to foster therefore is that of *"spirituality,"* in accordance with the typical charism of each Institute. In religious consecration, the intimacy, richness and stability of a special link with the Holy Spirit are at the root of all things.

God's presence becomes transparent when the religious becomes the sign and bearer of his supernatural love. Being a "minister" of divine charity is the source of service: the indissolubility of mission and consecration does not take the primacy from consecration, as the providential initiative of God who sends: "I who chose you and appointed you to go and bear fruit that will remain" (Jn 15:16).

What need there is today for authentic spirituality! Many people, including believers, feel lost and almost overwhelmed by the ephemeral, by indifference, relativism, individualism, the lack of transcendence and the loss of the sense of sin, which seem to be typical of the culture of our time.

Fresh apostolic zeal is expected from religious Institutes; in other words they are expected to make their contribution to the demanding task of the new evangelization, not only as individuals but as communities.

If this is to happen, spiritual renewal is still the first and most vital task to which religious must devote themselves. I am convinced that the Church will draw real strength from this, and it will even enable effective solutions to be found for the vocations crisis that has become worrying in some parts of the world.

The Council fittingly recalled that the best ways to give a fresh impetus to religious Institutes "will be of no avail unless they are animated by a *spiritual renewal*, which must always be assigned primary importance even in the active ministry" (*Perfectae caritatis*, n. 2).

107. Another important aspect to be emphasized is the commitment of religious to the *new evangelization*, a great challenge in our century to which the whole community of the baptized is called.

Economic progress, the changing social and political contexts, young people's expectations and the radical changes taking place in people's mentalities demand from evangelizers and particularly from consecrated persons the capacity to proclaim Christ's truth in a "contemporary" way so that every person may know that Jesus is the Redeemer of man with his specific difficulties and concrete problems.

In this effort, which involves the entire Church, it will be necessary to deepen and to clarify the spiritual and apostolic relations that exist between religious and lay people, promoting new methods and new expressions of cooperation, to facilitate the proclamation of Christ in our time.

108. Finally, it is necessary to remember that religious charisms are special gifts of the Spirit *for the People of God.*

The Extraordinary Synod of 1985 — twenty years after Vatican II — recalled that "the ecclesiology of communion is the central and fundamental idea of the Council's documents," and that it "cannot be reduced to purely organizational questions, or to problems which simply relate to powers" (*Final Report*, II, c. 1).

The encouragement of a more intense ecclesial communion between religious, clergy and lay people, intensifying a specific and multiform exchange of spiritual and apostolic values, will considerably help this ecclesiology of communion. It will more realistically link religious charisms to the individual Churches, where the vocation and mission of lay people and the diocesan clergy is expressed, bringing to them the dynamism and values by which religious communicate the universality of the Church.

109. Therefore I hope, beloved brothers and sisters, that the International Congress on "consecrated life today" may help you and the Institutes you represent here to see your presence as a precious gift from God to his Church and to the whole world.

The founders were able to incarnate the Gospel message in their time with courage and holiness. Faithful to the inspiration of the Spirit, their spiritual children must continue this witness in time, imitating their creativity with a mature fidelity to the original charism, constantly alert to the needs of the present moment.

May Mary, Queen of Virgins, concrete model of consecrated life, guide you and accompany you in this difficult and enormous task of renewal, and may she intercede for the good outcome of the next Synod.

I ask you, Immaculate Virgin, supreme model of faithful obedience, to revive in the Church the witness of the evangelical counsels, so that all may see the beauty of the Christian countenance in the spirit of the beatitudes.

Therefore, Mary most holy, help pastors too, so that they may have a vision and appreciation of consecrated life that reinforces its presence and mission among the People of God.

With these wishes, beloved brothers and sisters, I again assure you that I will constantly remember you to the Lord, as I impart a special apostolic blessing to support you in your daily effort to follow Christ, chaste, poor and obedient.

17

TO RELIGIOUS, MEMBERS OF
SECULAR INSTITUTES AND SOCIETIES
OF APOSTOLIC LIFE, IN ROME

February 2, 1994

110. *"Lift up, O gates, your lintels; reach up, you ancient portals, that the king of glory may come in!"* (Ps24[23]:7).

With these words from the psalm, the liturgy of today's feast *hails Jesus,* born in Bethlehem, as *he crossed the threshold of the Temple of Jerusalem for the first time.* Forty days after his birth, Mary and Joseph presented him in the Temple in accordance with the Law of Moses, "Every firstborn male shall be consecrated to the Lord" (Lk 2:23; cf. Ex 13:2,12).

The evangelist Luke draws attention to Jesus' parents' faithful observance of the law of the Lord that recommended the presentation of the newborn child and prescribed the purification of the mother. However, the Word of God does not mean to call our attention to these rites, but to the mystery of the Temple that today welcomes the One promised by the old Covenant and awaited by the prophets. *The Temple was destined for him.* The day was to come when he would enter it as the "Messenger of the Covenant" (cf. Mal 3:1) and would be revealed as "a light for revelation to the Gentiles and glory for your people (of God) Israel" (Lk 2:32).

111. Today's feast day is *like a great anticipation:* it anticipates Easter. In fact in the texts and liturgical symbols we glimpse, almost as a solemn messianic

proclamation, all that is to be fulfilled at the consummation of Jesus' mission in the mystery of his Passover. All those present in the Temple of Jerusalem witnessed almost unawares this anticipation of the Passover of the new Covenant: in other words, an event that was now close in the mysterious Child, an event that would give new meaning to everything.

The doors of the sanctuary opened to the wondrous king, who was "destined for the fall and rise of many in Israel, and to be a sign that will be contradicted" (Lk 2:34).

At the time, nothing revealed his kingship. That forty day-old infant was an ordinary child, the son of poor parents. Those who were closest knew that he was born in a stable near Bethlehem. They remembered the heavenly singing and the shepherds' visit, but how could even those who were closest, even Mary and Joseph, imagine that in the words of the Letter to the Hebrews, this child *was destined to help the descendants of Abraham, to be the only high priest before God* to expiate the sins of the world (cf. Heb 2:16-17)?

112. Actually, the infant's presentation in the Temple as one of the firstborn of Israel's families was precisely a sign of this: it was the proclamation of all the experiences, sufferings and trials to which he himself would submit, to come to the rescue of humanity, of those who are very often harshly tried by life.

It was to be Jesus, the merciful, the one and eternal Priest of God's new, unchanging Covenant with humanity, who would reveal the divine mercy. He would reveal the Father who "so loved the world" (Jn 3:16). He, the light, the light that enlightens every man, in the successive phases of history.

But this is why, always and in every age, Christ becomes the "sign of contradiction" (Lk 2:34). On that day, Mary, a young mother who bore him in her arms, was in a singular way to share in his suffering: the Virgin's soul was to be pierced and her *suffering together with the Redeemer would bring truth to the hearts of mankind* (cf. Lk 2:35).

113.   Thus the Temple of Jerusalem became the *scene of the messianic event.* After the night of Bethlehem, here was the first eloquent manifestation of the unmistakable mystery of the divine Birth. It was a revelation from the depths of the old Covenant.

Indeed, who was Simeon, whose words inspired by the Holy Spirit echoed beneath the vault of the Temple in Jerusalem? He was one of those who awaited "the consolation of Israel," whose expectation was filled with unshakable faith (cf. Lk 2:25). Simeon lived with the certainty that he would not die before he had seen the Messiah of the Lord: a certainty that came from the Holy Spirit (cf. *ibid.,* 2:26).

And who was Anna, the daughter of Phanuel? An elderly widow, described in the Gospel as a "prophetess," who never left the Temple and served God by fasting and praying night and day (cf. *ibid.,* 2:36-37).

114.   The figures who took part in the event we are commemorating today are all included in one great symbol: *the symbol of the Temple,* the Temple of Jerusalem, built by Solomon, whose pinnacles gave direction to the prayer of every generation of Israel. The sanctuary was in fact the fulfillment of the peoples' aspirations in the wilderness as they journeyed towards the promised land, and it expresses great expectation. *The whole of today's liturgy speaks of this expectation.*

In fact, the role of the Temple in Jerusalem is not confined to the old Covenant. *From the very beginning, its true meaning was the expectation of the Messiah:* built by men for the glory of the true God, the temple was to give way to another Temple that God himself was to build there, in Jerusalem.

Today, the One who says he is fulfilling its destiny and must "rebuild" it has come to the Temple. One day, while he was teaching in the Temple, Jesus was to say that this building, built by human hands, pulled down by invaders and rebuilt, would be pulled down again, but this last destruction *would indicate the beginning of an indestructible Temple.* After his resurrection, the disciples would understand that *he called his body a "Temple"* (cf. Jn 2:20-21).

115. Today then, dear brothers and sisters, we are living *a unique revelation of the mystery of the Temple,* a unique mystery: Christ himself. The sanctuary, including this basilica, *should not serve so much for worship as for holiness.* Everything to do with blessing, particularly with the dedication of sacred buildings, even in the new Covenant, *expresses the holiness of God,* who offers himself to man in Jesus and in the Holy Spirit.

The sanctifying work of God transforms temples made by human hands, but *its most appropriate place is man himself.* The consecration of buildings, even though architecturally magnificent, is a symbol of the sanctity that man draws from God through Christ. Through Christ, every person, man or woman, is called to become a living temple in the Holy Spirit: a temple in which God really dwells. Jesus spoke of such a spiritual temple in his conversation with the Samaritan woman, showing who the real worshippers of God were, those, that is, who glorify him "in Spirit and truth" (cf. Jn 4:23-24).

116. Saint Peter's Basilica rejoices in your presence today, dear brothers and sisters, who, coming from *different communities,* represent the world of *consecrated persons.* It is a beautiful tradition that you are precisely the ones to form *the holy assembly at this solemn*

celebration of Christ, the "light of the nations." In your hands you bear lighted candles, in your hearts the light of Christ, spiritually united with all your consecrated brothers and sisters in every corner of the world: you are the *Church's* irreplaceable, priceless *treasure.*

117. The history of Christianity confirms the value of your religious vocation: down the ages you have especially been linked with the spread of the Gospel's saving power among peoples and nations, on the European continent and then in the New World, in Africa and in the Far East.

We would especially like to remember that fact this year, when *the assembly of the Synod of Bishops dedicated to consecrated life in the Church* is to take place. We must remember it to glorify the Lord and to pray that such an important vocation, together with that of the family, *may not be stifled* in any way in our time, nor in the third millennium that is now approaching.

118. Today's Eucharistic celebration gathers consecrated people who work in Rome; but with our minds and hearts, we are united with the members of religious Orders and Congregations as well as of secular Institutes throughout the whole world, and above all with those who are giving Christ a *special witness*, paying for it with enormous sacrifices, even to the point of martyrdom. (...)

May Christ, the light of the world, be glorified in you dear brothers and sisters! May Christ, the sign of contradiction for this world, be glorified! Every person lives in him: in him, each person becomes the glory of God, as Saint Irenaeus teaches (cf. *Adv. haer.* 4, 20, 7). *You are the Epiphany of this truth.* This is why you are so loved in the Church and spread great hope among humanity. Today, in a particular way, we beg the Lord that the Gospel leaven of your vocation may reach more and more hearts of young men and women, and encourage them to consecrate themselves without reserve to the service of the Kingdom.

119. I say this also thinking of the other people present who have come for the Wednesday General Audience. Certainly, many of them know consecrated people, they realize the value of this personal consecration in the Church, they owe so much to the men and women religious who are working in the clinics, schools, and in the various surroundings of each nation, throughout the world. Today I would like to ask these guests at our General Audience, which is dedicated to religious life, to pray for all the consecrated people of the world, and to pray for vocations. Perhaps this prayer will inspire vocations in the hearts of young people.

120. Together with Mary and Joseph, today we are making a spiritual pilgrimage to the Temple in Jerusalem, *the city of the great meeting*, and with the liturgy we say: "Lift up, O gates...." All those who belong in faith to the children of Abraham find a common reference point in you. All desire that it should become *a meaningful center of peace*, so that — in accordance with the prophetic words of Revelation — God may wipe away every tear from the eyes of mankind (cf. Rv 21:4); and may that wall, for centuries a vestige of the ancient Temple of Solomon, cease to be the "Wailing Wall" and become a place of peace and reconciliation for believers in the one true God.

121. Today we go on pilgrimage to that city, especially we who have drawn inspiration for our whole life from the mystery of Christ: a life totally dedicated to the Kingdom of God. Our pilgrimage culminates in communion with the Body and Blood that the eternal Son of

God took upon himself by becoming man, that he might present himself to the Father in the flesh of his humanity, as a perfect spiritual sacrifice, thus fulfilling the Covenant God made with Abraham, our Father in faith, and brought to perfection in Christ (cf. Rom 4:16).

The Bishop of Rome looks lovingly towards Jerusalem; from there Simon Peter, his first predecessor, set out for Rome, spurred by his apostolic vocation: after him, the Apostle Paul also set out.

At the close of the second millennium, the successor of Peter kneels in the very places that were sanctified by the living God. As a pilgrim across the world, through cities, countries, continents, he remains in communion with the divine light that shone precisely there two thousand years ago, in the land that is truly holy, to enlighten the nations and peoples of the whole world; to enlighten us, dearly beloved.

18

MESSAGE TO PARTICIPANTS IN THE FIRST CONTINENTAL LATIN AMERICAN CONGRESS ON VOCATIONS

February 2, 1994

122. Dear brothers in the episcopate, beloved priests, religious and lay people,

In my *Message* this year for the *World Day of Prayer for Vocations*, I reminded the whole Church of the ecclesial event which you are preparing to celebrate: the *First Continental Latin American Congress on Vocations* in Itaici-São Paulo, Brazil, next May 23-27. I wanted to mention it because of its importance and so that the entire ecclesial community might express their solidarity and accompany you with spiritual closeness and fervent prayer, around Mary, the Mother of Jesus.

This is the first Congress in Latin America at a continental level and it inaugurates a series that, with God's help, will take place in the various continents where the Church is a sacrament of unity and the herald of Christ's message to peoples. I appreciated your keen interest in welcoming the Holy See's proposal that the Congress should be celebrated on the so-called "Continent of Hope."

123. The commemoration of the fifth centenary of the arrival of the Gospel in the New World is still recent. Within the framework of this event, the Latin American pastors — who gathered at the Fourth General Conference of the Latin American Episcopate in Santo Domingo to discuss the topic "the new evangelization, human development, Christian culture: 'Jesus Christ,

the same yesterday, today and forever'" — adopted the mission of renewed evangelizing action throughout the continent with strength and great hope. The present Congress fits into this context. Thus, in order to fulfill the mission of the new evangelization of the Latin American peoples, it is essential "to promote a vigorous vocations apostolate" (*Conclusions,* Santo Domingo, n. 293; cf. nn. 79-82).

I am convinced that this ecclesial meeting will prove to be for you and for the whole Church a special blessing of the Lord, Master of the harvest, who expects a generous response, thus promoting many holy vocations to the priesthood, to the consecrated life and to other forms of special Gospel commitment.

It should also be pointed out that this Congress is an eloquent gesture of ecclesial communion. In fact, right from the start it was intended to be the expression of co-responsibility and close collaboration between the Apostolic See, the Latin American Episcopal Council (CELAM) and the Latin American Confederation of Religious (CLAR). With this message, I wish to strengthen your resolve to work together to foster the pastoral care of vocations and to urge you, at the same time and with suitable initiatives, to encourage the Christian families and all the faithful to participate in this task, which is so important for the Church.

1. Latin America in the present day

124. You know well, dear brothers and sisters, that Latin America is experiencing a particularly vital moment in its history. Yours is a young continent full of promise, but it is facing tough challenges that demand from everyone a decisive will to overcome them. Its peoples long for freedom, for greater recognition of their dignity and for increased participation in the sociopolitical sector and in the ecclesial community

itself. Its features, described vividly and eloquently by the bishops in the documents of Puebla and Santo Domingo (cf. *Puebla*, nn. 31-37; *Santo Domingo*, n. 178), reflect the challenges and problems of those who are valiantly journeying towards the future. But on the distressed face of each individual and likewise on the face of Latin America as a whole, the light of hope and the desire for better times is also apparent.

The Church makes America's broad path her own, as she continues to proclaim and witness to the great love of Christ, the Redeemer of mankind and Savior of the world, who is present in her. Pastors, religious communities and committed lay people accompany her with faith and hope in parishes, schools, hospitals, missions and many other pastoral initiatives among the poor and marginalized, among youth and adults, in the various sociocultural categories of the people (cf. *Evangelii nuntiandi*, n. 69). The mission of evangelizers is constantly to kindle hope with the light and strength that come from the Lord, inspired by the urgency to make it shine forth in "the centers where a new humanity... is emerging" (*Redemptoris missio*, n. 37).

125.   The Church is aware of the enormous challenge to her mission presented by the present time. She knows, even in her weakness, that she is the harbinger of the hope for new life to which the Latin American people aspires and that it can only come from Christ, the Lord of Life. This is why she feels a pressing need for more "laborers for his harvest" (cf. Mt 9:38): men and women religious, people consecrated in the secular Institutes and committed lay people, to dedicate the best of their energy and their whole life to being the creators and symbols of Gospel hope.

We are pleased to note that over the past few years an increasing number of vocations have surfaced in the heart of those Christian homes that are deeply rooted in the faith. Diocesan seminaries and religious communities have witnessed growth in the number of their members, which is most encouraging. Through the witness of a Church which serves and is close to the people, the Lord has raised up men and women who wish to dedicate their whole life to Christ's cause. Furthermore, in communities radiant with strengthened Gospel values, he has increased the ardent wish of many young people to follow him more closely. How could we not thank God for this consoling fact!

126.   At the same time, however, the continent's pastoral needs have grown and the number of priests, religious and other consecrated people working in Latin America is altogether insufficient to meet the urgent need for pastoral care.

It is surprising to note that the greatest shortage of priests is found precisely in Latin America, the continent with the highest percentage of Catholics in proportion to its total population, and, as statistics show, with the greatest number of Catholics in the world. Gospel workers are needed in the suburbs of the great cities, in the rural areas, among the inhabitants of the mountainous regions of the Andes and in the immense jungles. There is a shortage of servants of the Good News who are dedicated to youth, to families, to the elderly and sick, to workers, intellectuals, the builders of society, as well as to the poorest and most marginalized. There is an urgent need for the presence of a greater number of priests and religious in parishes, apostolic movements, basic ecclesial communities, schools and universities, and in many other sectors, as I emphasized in the Encyclical *Redemptoris missio* (cf. n. 37). On the other hand, looking at the broad horizon of the universal mission entrusted to the Church, there is also a shortage of men and women missionaries to go beyond your frontiers to proclaim to the ends of the earth the "inscrutable riches of Christ" (Eph 3:8; *Conclusions*, Santo Domingo, nn. 121-125).

2. Effective pastoral care of vocations is required

127. For all these reasons, there is an increasingly urgent need for a renewed vocations apostolate. In the first place, it should be conceived as a necessary dimension of the overall or global pastoral program, and at the same time, as a specific field of action for guiding or inspiring the discernment and growth of a vocational response from those called by the Lord to follow him. No pastoral action can ever forget that education in the faith also means developing the vocational dynamism that is part of Christian life. Being Christian is already in itself a vocation, a call: the highest vocation, the source and basis of any specific "following of Christ" within the ecclesial community.

It is therefore necessary to develop the vocational dimension of baptismal life from childhood. Throughout his development, the Christian needs to be increasingly accustomed to hearing the voice of God calling him; he needs increasingly to open his heart to welcome his invitation; he must be ever more willing to walk the way of the Lord who precedes us in the proclamation of his Kingdom. Thus the protection of Christian mothers and the warmth and constant prayer in believing homes teach children and young people to value their life as a call to give and to give of themselves. "The pastoral care of vocations finds its first and natural setting in the family," I said in my Message for World Day of Prayer for Vocations this year.[1] Yes, the family is called to give children the joyful experience of a Christian vocation, preparing itself to receive as a very precious gift the call of some of their children to the priestly ministry or the consecrated life.

–
[1] cf. p.141

128.   There is no doubt, however, that the most important and favorable period in which to hear, discern and follow the Lord's voice is youth, the age when
the human person is more generously open to the ideal
of making a total gift of self. The Gospel tells how Jesus,
in multiplying the loaves to appease the hunger of the
people who had followed him, needed the generosity of
a boy who offered all he had, his barley loaves and his
fish (cf. Jn 6:9); and how in Galilee he attracted John and
Andrew, who followed him, saw where he was staying
and stayed with him that day (cf. Jn 1:39).

Do not tire then of encouraging effective pastoral
care for youth, one rich in Gospel life and clearly
inviting them to consider a vocation: present youth with
an attractive experience of friendship with the Lord, a
solid catechetical formation and a responsible apostolic
commitment. Today's young people are capable of
generosity and they will be able to respond with a
generous "yes" to the Lord who is calling them.

3. With appropriate methods

129.   The problem of vocations affects the life of the
Church itself. Without sufficient *laborers for the
harvest* it is impossible to make the mandate of Christ —
which was the very reason for his existence and his
mission in history — a reality: "Go, therefore, and make
disciples of all nations..." (Mt 28:19), nor would it be
possible to renew the Eucharistic sacrifice each day: "Do
this in remembrance of me" (1 Cor 11:24), (*Pastores dabo
vobis*, n. 1).

Aware of the urgent call of the present time, I urge
you to demonstrate your concern as pastors in effective
programs and daring pastoral projects that give real
dynamism and coordination to what in this sector is
being done already in every diocese and in every country. It is to be hoped that the Continental Congress

which you will be celebrating will provide fresh incentive to make good the promise that is emerging.

130. I also wished to stress several elements which must be taken into account in programs for the pastoral care of vocations:

— The prerequisite of the vocations apostolate is first and foremost a witness of authentic faith, joyful hope and active charity. We need ecclesial communities that truly strive to live fraternal communion, the fruit of participation in the Eucharist, persevering in prayer, assiduous in listening to the Word and in works of charity. Indeed, witness continues to be the most convincing force of attraction which the disciples of Christ have at their disposal.

— In addition, frequent and explicit prayers for vocations should be said in dioceses, parishes and communities of consecrated life. Promote Christian communities which are assiduous in prayer, conscious that they themselves, with their own efforts alone, will not be able to provide the vocations they need and, as a result, they must be always ready to welcome them, guide them and sustain them as a true gift from on high.

— The pastoral care of vocations implies and also demands that vocations be carefully and concretely followed up. This requires people who are spiritually, theologically and pedagogically trained, and who are dedicated to this important ecclesial mission, various and suitable places for welcome and support, satisfactory and thorough methods of Christian formation, discernment and vocational guidance, sincere and loyal collaboration between the various people in charge of the vocations apostolate in the different contexts and at the different ecclesial levels.

131. Dear brothers, these are a few considerations that come from my heart as a pastor, and which I place

in the hands of Mary, Mother and Queen of the Apostles, that she may intercede before her divine Son for the successful outcome of the Congress.

The Church in Latin America needs and hopes for numerous candidates with holy vocations who will devote their whole life to the new evangelization. May this prayer rise from the many shrines throughout your nations, from the ecclesial communities and from Christian families:

Lord Jesus Christ,

Sent by the Father and anointed by the Spirit, who entrusted your disciples with the proclamation of salvation, that it might spread to the ends of the earth and to the end of time, raise up a new springtime of vocations in Latin America.

You, who know each by name and have the words of eternal life, renew in the Continent of Hope the invitation to leave everything and follow you, so that many young people may commit themselves to you in the priestly ministry or in the consecrated life, dedicating themselves without reserve to the service of the Gospel.

You, who entrust the words of the Father to your friends, be the only Lord and Master of all those you call.

Shower the gifts of the Spirit upon the ecclesial communities, so that a new generation of apostles may proclaim your Resurrection to all people and gather them into your Church.

Renew in all the baptized the pressing call to the new evangelization, so that they may be witnesses of your Truth and your Life among the men and women of our time.

We ask this of you through the intercession of the Virgin Mary, model of total dedication to your service and Mother of all those called to be the apostles of your kingdom. Amen.

With my apostolic blessing.

19

TO THE GENERAL CHAPTER OF THE BROTHERS OF CHRISTIAN INSTRUCTION OF PLOERMEL

March 28, 1994

132.   On the occasion of your General Chapter, I am pleased to express to you, to the capitulars, and to all the Brothers of Christian Instruction, my great respect for your Institute and your vocation as religious educators.

Generations of Brothers have put into practice the specific charism which took shape under the vigorous inspiration of your founders, Venerable Jean-Marie de La Mennais and Father Gabriel Deshayes. Today your sessions have enabled you to draw up the necessary guidelines to carry out your mission according to the present situation.

One important aspect of your state is to unite religious life with a professional activity that is integrated into properly ecclesial tasks. You cannot separate the practice of your teaching role from your personal consecration. This is certainly an irreplaceable contribution of teaching brothers in the Church.

Today you are often called to live in a less homogenous environment than in the past, and in several of the countries where you work your witness is aimed at generations of youth who come from backgrounds with little or no religious preparation or incentive to seek a living faith. This situation requires from you a constantly renewed pedagogical effort so that the Christian message and basic human and moral values may be convincingly presented and accepted by young people, who live in a society where they are sometimes forced to go against the tide.

133.   However, you must first be authentic consecrated persons. In your personal spiritual life and in your fraternal community life, you find the strength to be faithful to your vocation and to be the kind of witnesses that Christ wanted. As I address you on the eve of the Easter Triduum, Jesus' words in the Upper Room naturally spring to my mind: "This is how all will know that you are my disciples, if you have love for one another" (Jn 13:35). This reminds us in a word that an ecclesial service can be authentic only if it is based on the disciples' loving communion in Christ.

Your religious life as a community, as well as your integration into the particular Churches of the countries where you live, are an essential source that enables you to be the evangelizers whom young people need. Your way of giving yourselves to the Lord for the people he loves, through a life of chastity, poverty and obedience, is as valuable as the best teaching methods in transmitting the Christian message, which is your task. In fact, people of our time, especially youth, are often more sensitive to witness than to teaching. Through your openness of spirit, your sense of acceptance and the simplicity of your life, may people see you as men imbued with the life-giving presence of the Redeemer and inspired by hope that never disappoints!

134.   Your Congregation's charism has led you to found numerous schools. Continue to give these institutions the best of yourselves so that they may be true reference points for youth and their families. Be creative, in order to provide your educational communities with a dynamic spirit so that they are seen as privileged places where the Church fulfills her mission to awaken people to faith and to give witness to her immense

respect for the human person who is called to develop in the sight of God.

I know of your preferential concern to serve the poorest and for this I am glad. Through your availability, be welcoming to all, wherever you may be. Associate with your apostolate the teachers who work with you, your pupils, their families and other Christians who share your concern as teachers and evangelizers.

Dear Brothers, ever since its foundation, your Congregation has played a notable part in the mission *ad gentes*. Very early on, the Brothers devoted themselves to the service of peoples who were beginning to accept the Good News of Christ. Today you are generously continuing that missionary presence. The Church is extremely grateful to the religious who contribute all their resources to strengthening the young Churches and to developing numerous countries, through the training imparted to children and adolescents. I sincerely appreciate the fact that you have responded to new calls, despite the reduction in your numbers.

135. A General Chapter is not only an occasion to adapt, to review the organization and ways of life, but also and primarily to take a fresh look at the profound unity of a vocation, its raison d'être and its role in the Church's mission as it is expressed in our time. I am also thinking of your many elderly Brothers. Their specific role should be recognized; perhaps they should be entrusted with new tasks. With the wisdom of their experience and their spiritual life, they certainly exercise a beneficial influence on the life of the Congregation as a whole.

I know that you are worried by the question of recruitment. Do not neglect any effort to make young people attentive to the deep reasons for dedicating themselves to the service of the Lord in the religious life. Do not hesitate to propose the kind of life that makes you profoundly happy to young Christians who are open to the service of others and conscious of the need to live effectively the solidarity between the peoples of a country or of different countries. Let them discover through your enthusiasm the joy of giving themselves to Christ without reserve in a religious community, the better to share the gifts of God and to proclaim the Kingdom to come.

With you, Brother Superior General, and with the capitular Brothers, I invoke the Spirit of the Lord, that he may guide your decisions and assist those to whom you will entrust the leadership of your Congregation. In this season, when we are celebrating the mystery of the death and Resurrection of Christ the Savior, I impart to you and all your Brothers my affectionate blessing.

20

MESSAGE FOR THE WORLD DAY OF PRAYER FOR VOCATIONS

April 24, 1994

136.   The celebration of the World Day of Prayer for Vocations coincides, this year, with an important ecclesial event. It is the inauguration of the "First Continental Latin American Congress on Pastoral Care for Vocations of Special Consecration on the Continent of Hope."

This Assembly has set for itself an in-depth task of examining, encouraging and promoting vocations. As I express a keen appreciation for this pastoral initiative, which aims at the spiritual good not only of Latin America but of the whole Church, I call upon everyone to support it in common and confident prayer.

The World Day of Prayer takes place, besides, during the International Year of the Family. This affords the opportunity of calling attention to the close relationship which exists between family, education and vocation, and particularly between family and priestly and religious vocations.

In addressing myself to Christian families, I wish thereby to confirm them in their mission of educating the young generations, which are the hope and future of the Church.

1. "This is a great mystery" (Eph 5:32).

137.   In spite of profound historical changes, the family remains the most complete and the richest school of humanity, in which one lives the most significant experience of unselfish love, fidelity, mutual respect

and the defense of life. Its particular task is to protect and hand on virtues and values, by means of the education of the children, in such a way as to build up and promote the good of individuals and of the community.

This same responsibility involves, with greater reason, the Christian family, because its members, already consecrated and sanctified in virtue of their baptism, are called to a particular apostolic vocation by the sacrament of matrimony (cf. *Familiaris consortio*, nn. 52, 54).

The family, to the extent to which it becomes conscious of this singular vocation and measures up to it, becomes a community of sanctification in which one learns to live meekness, justice, mercy, chastity, peace, purity of heart (cf. Eph 4:1-4; *Familiaris consortio*, n. 21). It becomes, in other words, what Saint John Chrysostom called "the domestic church," that is, a place in which Jesus Christ lives and works for the salvation of men and for the growth of the Kingdom of God. The members of the family, called to faith and to eternal life, are "sharers in the divine nature" (2 Pt 1:4), they are nourished at the table of the Word of God and of the sacraments, and they express themselves in that evangelical way of thinking and acting which opens them up to a life of holiness on earth and of eternal happiness in heaven (cf. Eph 1:4-5).

138. Christian parents, demonstrating a loving care for their children from their earliest years, communicate to them, by word and example, a sincere and lived relationship with God, made up of love, fidelity, prayer and obedience (cf. *Lumen gentium*, n. 35; *Apostolicam actuositatem*, n. 11). In this way, parents encourage the holiness of their children and render their hearts docile to the voice of the Good Shepherd, who calls every man to follow him and to seek first the Kingdom of God.

In the light of this perspective of divine grace and human responsibility, the family can be considered a "garden" or a "first seminary" in which the seeds of vocation, which God sows generously, are able to blossom and grow to full maturity (cf. *Optatam totius*, n. 2).

2. "Do not conform yourself to this age" (Rom 12:2).

The task of Christian parents is as important as it is sensitive, because they are called to prepare, cultivate and protect the vocations which God stirs up in their family. They must, therefore, enrich themselves and their family with spiritual and moral values, such as a deep and convinced religious spirit, an apostolic and ecclesial consciousness, and a clear idea of what a vocation is.

In fact, for every family, the decisive step to be taken is that of accepting the Lord Jesus as the center and pattern of life, and in him and with him, becoming conscious of being the privileged place for authentic vocational growth.

139.   The family will fulfill this task if it is constant in its commitment and if it relies always on the grace of God. For Saint Paul declares that "God is the one who, for his good purpose, works ... both the will and the deed" (Phil 2:13), and that "the One who began a good work ... will continue to complete it until the day of Christ Jesus" (*ibid.*, 1:6).

But what happens when the family lets itself become involved in consumerism, hedonism and secularism, which upset and block the fulfillment of God's plan?

How sad it is to learn of situations, unfortunately numerous, of families overwhelmed by such phenomena and of the devastating effects! This is certainly one of the greatest concerns of the Christian community. It is above all the families themselves who pay the price of the widespread disorder of ideas and of moral behavior. But the Church also suffers from this, just as the entire society feels its effects.

How can children, morally rendered orphans, without educators and without models, grow in their esteem for human and Christian values? How can those seeds of vocations, which the Holy Spirit continues to put into the hearts of the young generations, develop in such a climate?

140. The strength and stability of the fabric of the Christian family represent the primary condition for the growth and maturation of consecrated vocations, and they constitute the most pertinent response to the crisis of vocations. As I wrote in the Exhortation *Familiaris consortio*: "Every local Church and, in more particular terms, every parochial community must become more vividly aware of the grace and responsibility that it receives from the Lord, so that it might promote the pastoral care of the family. No plan for organized pastoral work at any level must ever fail to take into consideration the pastoral area of the family" (n. 70).

3. "Ask the Master of the harvest, therefore, to send out laborers for his harvest" (Mt 9:38).

The pastoral care of vocations finds its first and natural setting in the family. Indeed, parents should know how to welcome as a grace the gift which God gives them in calling one of their sons or daughters to the priesthood or religious life. Such a grace must be asked for in prayer and received actively, by means of an education which allows the young people to perceive all the richness and joy of consecrating oneself to God.

Parents who welcome the call of a son or daughter to a special consecration for the Kingdom of God with a sense of gratitude and joy, receive a special sign of the spiritual fruitfulness of their union, as they see it enriched by the experience of love lived out in celibacy and virginity.

These parents discover with amazement that the gift of their love is, as it were, multiplied, thanks to the vocation of their children, beyond the limited dimensions of human love.

To bring families to the awareness of this important aspect of their mission requires a pastoral activity aimed at leading spouses and parents to be "witnesses and cooperators of the fruitfulness of mother Church, as a sign of, and a share in that love with which Christ loved his bride and gave himself for her" (*Lumen gentium*, n. 41).

The family is the natural "nursery" of vocations. Pastoral care of the family, therefore, should direct a very special attention to the properly vocational aspect of its task.

4. "Let the one who has responsibility in the community show care and diligence" (Rom 12:8).

141. *Walking together, following Christ, towards the Father* is the most appropriate vocational program. If priests, religious men and women, missionaries and committed laity concern themselves with the family and intensify the forms of dialogue and of a common seeking to live the Gospel, the family will be enriched with those values which will help it to be the first "seminary" of vocations and of consecrated life.

Let priests, diocesan and religious, take to heart the problems of family life, so that, by means of the proclamation of the Gospel, they might give light to Christian spouses about their peculiar responsibilities, and thus the parents, well formed in the faith, will be able to guide their sons and daughters who might be called to give themselves unreservedly to God.

Let all consecrated persons, who are particularly close to and accepted by families because of their apostolic service in schools, hospitals, institutions of assistance and parishes, offer joyful witness of their total gift to Christ. Let them, with their lives lived according to the vows of poverty, chastity and obedience, be a sign of and call to eternal values for Christian spouses.

Let the parish community sense itself responsible for this mission to the family and support it with long-term projects, without being too concerned about immediate results.

I entrust to committed Christians, catechists and young couples the task of catechesis in the family. With their generous and faithful service may they help children to have their first taste of a religious and ecclesial experience.

My thought goes in a special way towards my *venerable brothers in the episcopate,* as the ones first responsible for the promotion of vocations, and I recommend that they make every effort to see to it that the pastoral care of vocations be systematically joined with that of the family.

Let us pray

142. *O Holy Family of Nazareth, community of love of Jesus, Mary and Joseph, model and ideal of every Christian family, to you we entrust our families.*

Open the heart of every family to the faith, to welcoming the word of God, to Christian witness, so that it become a source of new and holy vocations.

Touch the hearts of parents, so that with prompt charity, wise care, and loving devotion they be for their sons and daughters sure guides towards spiritual and eternal values.

Stir up in the hearts of young people a right con-science and a free will, so that growing in "wisdom, age and grace," they might welcome generously the gift of a divine vocation.

Holy Family of Nazareth, grant that all of us, contem-plating and imitating the assiduous prayer, generous obedi-ence, dignified poverty and virginal purity lived out in your midst, might set about fulfilling the will of God and accompa-nying with farsighted sensitivity those among us who are called to follow more closely the Lord Jesus, who "has given himself for us" (cf. Gal 2:20). Amen!

21

TO THE CAPUCHIN FRANCISCANS

July 1, 1994

143.   I am pleased today to meet you who are taking part in your General Chapter, "the greatest sign of union and solidarity of the whole Capuchin fraternity gathered together in its representatives," as is written in your Constitutions (16, 1).

With affection I greet the newly-elected Minister General, Father John Corriveau, to whom I express my best wishes for success in the new work of governance to which he has been called. My thoughts in particular turn to Father Flavio Roberto Carraro, who for twelve years was the leader of your Order, and I pray that he may receive an abundant reward of grace and peace for the dedication which he gave to his work.

Every Chapter benefits the Order and is a necessary time of reflection not only on the profound meaning of its own specific vocations, but also on the human situations which challenge the Franciscan fraternity to read and welcome the "signs of the times" (cf. Mt 16:1-3; Lk 12:54-57), the voice of God for the Institute.

144.   Certainly there is no need for me to remind you that this meeting is being held at a very significant time for the Church in general and in a very special way for those called to the consecrated life. The forthcoming Ordinary General Assembly of the Synod of Bishops, the theme of which is to be "The Consecrated Life and its Role in the Church and in the World," is indeed a special stimulus for the whole People of God to reflect on the inestimable gift which the Spirit has made, and continues to make, to the Church of Christ through the

charism of the consecrated life. The six-year interval between Chapters which is now beginning also is of special historical importance for the ecclesial Community, which is preparing for the celebration of the second millennium of the Incarnation of Jesus Christ.

145.   In this context the mission of the believer, and of every religious especially, is *to bear witness to the Absolute*, even amid the tragic consequences caused by the "absence of God" found in broad sectors of today's society. This means above all that the Capuchin must live in union with the Lord, experiencing God's presence in his own life.

Prayer and contemplation: that is the primary task you must fulfill, following the shining example of Saint Francis and so many other masters of your long tradition. From intimate communion with the divine Trinity flows the fraternal love which you are called to live first of all with one another ("By this they will know...": Jn 13:35). Then you can be ready to live for others, especially for the poor, as you are continuously reminded by your Constitutions and the documents of your Order. Fraternity is a value which Saint Francis himself, moved by the Holy Spirit, inculcated in his first companions in order to heal the divided society of his day. Today you want to propose this life-style anew in an age in which the virus of division and individualism is particularly rampant. Therefore, be examples of fraternity and harmony: within your communities offer your witness as brothers living together in peace, in prayer, true charity, mutual forgiveness, poverty and acceptance.

146.   What is necessary for this is a *creative and concrete fidelity to your Capuchin Franciscan charism,* which is recognized increasingly in the light of the teaching and example of your holy Founder, Francis of Assisi. Commit yourselves to continuing his work and Gospel

witness, seeking areas for your presence, witness and apostolic service that satisfy the ever new demands of people today.

I spoke of *creative fidelity*, thus meaning to refer to the need for an attentive reading of the signs of the times in order to discover what the Holy Spirit is suggesting to today's Christians. This reading is to be done with the sensitivity of the Poverello of Assisi himself, who was led to respond to the demands of the radical nature of the Gospel with a new form of the consecrated life. Francis' openness and availability will free you from both the risk of immobility and the temptation of facile acquiescence to changing fashion.

147. Furthermore, *your fidelity must be concrete*: Saint Francis urged his friars to witness to Christ *"plus exemplo quam verbo"* (more by example than by word). From this standpoint it is necessary, both in concern for vocations and in the initial and ongoing formation of the friars, to promote the *quality* of the consecrated life rather than the *quantity* of consecrated persons. You should be more concerned to be authentic *witnesses of God* and of *Gospel brotherhood:* you, dear Capuchins, are an *Ordo Fratrum* (Order of brothers), called to preserve and strengthen your traditional *nearness to people* through a wise process of inculturation.

In order to *be close* to people you must strive through study, reflection and prayer to understand in the light of the Gospel the problems and needs they are experiencing today. Without solid doctrine there is the risk of working in vain.

The commitment to trying to satisfy the profound needs of our world will also lead you to be *creative.* Dearly beloved, have this true prophetic orientation in helping the people of our times who, as far as moral values are concerned, are frequently groping in the dark. Work with young people, promote Bible groups and prayer communities. *Bring Christ to the world!* Bear him courageously. *Your Order has always given* a shining example of evangelization, especially through the practice of contact with the people, which is your distinguishing trait.

148. *Be missionaries!* The need for bringing the Gospel *ad gentes* is all the more compelling since there is a growing number of peoples who have not yet truly met the Lord Jesus. Instill missionary zeal in the young generations and the young jurisdictions of your Order, always keeping strong the ecclesial nature of your charism, in line with the "mandate" Saint Francis received from the Crucifix of San Damiano: "Go and repair my house." Francis did so in his day, and now it is your turn! The pastoral needs of one's native land are an insufficient reason not to leave one's country and go where God is leading.

Be apostles of peace, a gift of God that is all too often trampled underfoot by injustice and crime in a world which claims to be civilized and advanced.

The evangelical life truly lived and proclaimed will make you *prophets*, that is, men of God and God-bearers, true sons of the seraphic Father who, as one of his biographers wrote, was possessed of a "shining spirit of prophecy" (Ubertino da Casale, *Arbor vitae crucifixae Jesu*, V, 3). In his teaching and example you have a rich heritage to preserve: it will make you particularly prepared for the new evangelization in view of the imminent Jubilee Year of 2000.

149. Dear brothers, I would like to conclude by recalling a beautiful admonition found in your Constitutions, which reflects the wisdom of the Spirit who nourished the hearts of your fathers: "In the apostolate... be poor and humble, without claiming the ministry as your own, so that it will be clear to everyone that you

seek Jesus Christ alone; preserve that unity of fraternity which Christ wants to be so perfect that the world may recognize that the Son has been sent by the Father. In your fraternal life cultivate a spirit of prayer and study in order to be intimately united with the Savior and, moved by the Holy Spirit, always be generously ready to witness the Good News to the world" (*Const.*, 154, 3-4).

With these wishes I entrust the results of your Chapter to the motherly protection of Mary, the "faithful Virgin," that she may preserve in you a strong desire for fidelity to the evangelical and Franciscan vocation. I ask the "Queen of Apostles" to help you, like the first disciples, to experience the presence of Jesus Christ and an intimate union with him. I ask the "Queen of Prophets" to obtain for you the grace of being inwardly possessed by the Spirit of God, so that you may be effective instruments of salvation for your brothers and sisters. As I commend to your prayer the needs of the Church and thank you for the valuable service you offer to the Kingdom of God, I cordially impart the apostolic blessing to all those present and to your whole Order.

22

TO PRIESTS, RELIGIOUS AND SEMINARIANS IN ZAGREB (CROATIA)

September 10, 1994

150.   I am glad to be able to meet you in this cathedral, the spiritual center of the archdiocese. I cordially greet not only you who are present here, but all those who have been prevented from taking part in this moment of communion and prayer by work, their state of health or other difficulties. You are a chosen part of the People of God in Croatia, and it is therefore right that during the Pope's visit, room should be made especially for you.

Dear priests, dear religious, Cardinal Alojzije Stepinac, whose mortal remains are preserved in this cathedral used to call you the "pupil of his eyes." He was right, because you must be at the heart of the Church's solicitude since *her action in the world depends to a large extent on your ministry.* By virtue of sacred ordination and the mission you have received from your bishop, you are called to relive the service of Christ the Prophet, Priest and King among today's people.

151.   Not only the Church but *society too needs priests and people consecrated to God,* because — despite appearances to the contrary — today man feels the need for God with particular keenness. Material goods alone are not enough and man's heart is restless, continuously seeking what can give meaning and value to his life. *Priests are necessary to the world* because Christ is necessary. *People consecrated to God are necessary,* because man needs to be constantly reminded of the eternal and spiritual values.

You must always be deeply convinced that the future of the Church depends largely on holy priests and religious who are in love with Christ and full of zeal for their own brothers and sisters; priests and religious forming one heart and one mind with their bishops and their confrères; priests and religious committed to deepening God's word in study and in prayer, in order to draw from it guidance and support in their own consecrated life and in their daily apostolates.

All this cannot be improvised, it should be prepared gradually during the years at the seminary, and then constantly rediscovered and deepened. Thinking of priestly formation, I cannot omit here to greet with affection the seminarians present, the hope of the Church of the future.

Beloved, live your years at the seminary as a period of great *intimacy* with Christ. Learn to know his Heart, in order to become priests according to God's Heart, living and transparent images of the Good Shepherd.

152. A serious task weighs heavily on your shoulders, beloved priests and religious; *to reconcile men with God and among themselves*. It is a duty which is incumbent on you especially at this difficult historical moment when a senseless and cruel war has devastated the Balkans, scarring your homeland too and making deep furrows of hatred which only the love inspired by God's Spirit can pacify.

It is up to you priests, who during Mass live and re-present the sacrifice of Golgotha "in persona Christi," to be the convinced witnesses of him who, dying, did not hesitate to say: "Father, forgive them!" Looking at you, at the ministry of reconciliation which you exercise, but above all the example which you generously provide, your people will find the strength to *forgive*, and, where necessary, *to ask forgiveness*. This requires humility and open-mindedness, love for the truth and the quest for genuine peace. I entrust this demanding but indispensable task to you, the apostles of and witnesses to forgiveness and reconciliation.

153. Be faithful to your identity as priests and make the Eucharist, the liturgy, the sacraments and prayer the motivation of your apostolate, supported by the conviction that God's Spirit conquers evil, that his grace is stronger than human wickedness, that love and not hatred will have the final word.

In imitation of Christ, let *fidelity to celibacy* be resplendent in you, allowing you to devote yourselves without reserve to the service of the Lord and your neighbor. In this regard, I must praise the many priests and religious who, during the tragic moments of the recent war shared with their people the condition of refugees, adapting themselves to living in precarious and often humiliating situations. Continue, beloved, to be close to your faithful, so sorely tried that they need your affection and your generous ministry in order to withstand the discomforts of the present moment, and to keep their hope for a better future alive.

154. The clear conviction that human beings, regardless of the ethnic roots or nation to which they belong, *are all children of the same Father who is in heaven,* must be reflected in your words and behavior.

The ecumenical dialogue which you and your pastors have very much at heart should be seen in this perspective, even in the present difficult circumstances. Do not be discouraged in following this path desired by the Lord; he will be able to crown it in his own time with the desired results.

In the course of several centuries, remarkable examples of Croatian priests and religious have left an extraordinary spiritual heritage. I am thinking particularly of your two saints, the Franciscan Nicholas of Tavelic and the Capuchin, Leopold Bogdan Mandic. I am pleased today to be able to give Cardinal Franjo Kuharic, President of the Croatian Episcopal Conference, *a relic of Saint Leopold, a great saint of the sacrament of confession.* May this eminent son of your people also become, by this sign, an invitation to you all to carry out in your life what is the daily subject of your preaching.

155.   From the long list of men and women who distinguished themselves in our day in the exercise of Christian virtue, I would like to recall the Servants of God: Josip Lang, Auxiliary Bishop of Zagreb, the Franciscans Vendelin Vosnjak and Ante Antic, as well as Ivan Merz, a lay man actively involved in witnessing the Gospel in today's world. Nevertheless, the most prestigious figure is that of the *Archbishop and Cardinal, Alojzije Stepinac.* With his presence, work, courage and patience, with his silence, and finally, his death, he showed himself to be a true man of the Church, ready to make the supreme sacrifice, rather than deny the faith. In every circumstance, in freedom, in prison or under house arrest, he always watched as a true pastor over his flock; and when he realized that through adherence to political associations, there was a plan to divide the clergy and cut off the People of God from the Church of Rome, he did not hesitate to oppose it with all his might, paying with imprisonment for his courage.

At that dramatic time in your national history he reflected the most authentic tradition of your people who, from the very beginning of their conversion to Christ, have always professed deep communion with the See of Peter. I recognized this already in 1979, during the solemn Eucharistic celebration on the occasion of the national Croatian pilgrimage. At the time, recalling the words of Pope John VIII in his *Epistula ad populum et clerum Croatum* in which he wrote: "With open arms I clasp you to myself, and I welcome you with fatherly love," I emphasized "the Croatians' love and loyalty to the Roman Church, to the Chair of Saint Peter" (*Insegnamenti*, Vol. II/I, 1979, p. 1024 f.).

156. The new times require appropriate methods for evangelization. The establishment of the democratic regime in Croatia has opened up *new possibilities for pastoral activities* in the areas of teaching, the media, in spiritual assistance to the military, the sick and prisoners. You must make use of these with creativity, in full harmony with the bishops and with the rest of the diocesan and national presbyterate.

The precious contribution of the religious brothers fits into the context of this work of vigilant pastoral care to be accomplished in every sector. Opportunely involved, they can effectively contribute to the edification of the Christian community.

It is also becoming necessary and urgent to *promote a well trained laity* who will be able to work with you, especially in catechesis and social assistance, enabling you to dedicate more time to your specific ministerial activities.

157. I would now like to address a special word to *the sisters*. Beloved Sisters, I know very well your joyous witness of love for Christ and for your brothers and sisters, I know your hopes as well as your problems, and all you have suffered. I would like to express my appreciation for your work in the parishes as catechists, sacristans, organists; I appreciate your commitment to children and the elderly, and your work in the hospitals. I say to you: *persevere with joy* in the work of evangelization and in your witness to charity. The Lord is with you and also makes use of your service, all the more precious for being hidden, to continue his work of salvation among the peoples of this land so dear to him.

Lastly, I greet the *cloistered nuns in Croatia* with particular affection: the Poor Clares and the Discalced Carmelites, as well as the Benedictine nuns. Cardinal Stepinac did all he could to establish a monastery of Discalced Carmelites in Brezovica. He wanted the diocese to have *an oasis of prayer* from which constant prayers would be raised for priests, for religious and for the Croatian people. Dear cloistered nuns, be faithful to your original charism. You express the contemplative soul of the Church: persevere in your task as *vigilant guardians of the Absolute,* constantly in dialogue with God, to present him "the joys and hopes, the griefs and anxieties of the men of our time" (*Gaudium et spes,* n. 1) and to draw from him mercy and forgiveness to bestow upon so many brothers and sisters in difficulty. The clergy, the religious communities and the Croatian people have great need of your prayers and of your witness of life, centered totally on eternity.

158.   In this great cathedral which preserves the memory of so many illustrious men of your people, I remember with gratitude our worthy Cardinal Franjo Seper, whom I knew and esteemed. As pastor of this archdiocese and then as Prefect of the Congregation for the Doctrine of the Faith, he gave a valuable service to the Church.

Dear priests, seminarians and religious, in taking my leave I entrust you to Our Lady, whom the people of Croatia like to invoke as their own "Queen." A true relationship with Jesus Christ must be accompanied by a true devotion to Mary, his Mother and our most beloved Mother. May Mary go with you always and guide your steps in the service of the Church and the nation. With this wish, I wholeheartedly impart my blessing to you all, to your families and to the people entrusted to your pastoral care.

23

MESSAGE TO THE SUPERIOR GENERAL OF THE PASSIONISTS, FOR THE THIRD CENTENARY OF THE BIRTH OF SAINT PAUL OF THE CROSS

September 14, 1994

159. It is a great joy for me to participate in the celebrations announced by this Congregation in honor of its Founder, Saint Paul of the Cross, on the occasion of the third centenary of his birth, and I greatly appreciated the intention to solemnize this anniversary not only with public events, but even more with a community reflection on the witness which this great mystic and evangelizer of the eighteenth century has left to his spiritual children and to the Church.

The anniversary invites us to turn our gaze to the Passion of Jesus, upon which Saint Paul of the Cross centered his whole life and apostolate, first experiencing it mystically, then proclaiming it to others in preaching and spiritual direction. He had a deep understanding of the teaching, particularly vivid in John's Gospel, that Jesus' Passion is also his glorification, his exaltation, inasmuch as it is his obedient acceptance of the Father's infinite love and his sharing it with all men. In Jesus crucified, according to the expression in the Letter to the Colossians (cf. 1:15), he also saw the living image of the Father, the perfect icon of the invisible God. Some of the expressions with which he demonstrated his profound understanding of the mystery of the Cross are rightly famous: "Jesus' Passion is the greatest and most stupendous work of Divine Love" (*Letters*, II, 499); it is "Divine Love's miracle of miracles" (*ibid.*, 726). "From the sea of divine Charity," he used to say, "flows the sea of Jesus' Passion and these are two seas in one" (*ibid.*, 717). There was nothing so effective for him as the proclamation of the Passion of Jesus for converting hardened hearts.

160. The fundamental task for the Church in every age — and particularly in our time — is to introduce mankind to Christ, to the paschal mystery, which through the Cross and death, leads to the resurrection. In this mystery Christ is united with every man, reveals the face of his Father to him and fully reveals man to himself (cf. *Redemptor hominis,* nn. 10-13). In my Apostolic Letter *Salvifici doloris* on the Christian meaning of human suffering — a document that is particularly close to the charism of this Congregation — I dwelt on the mystery of the Cross in relation to the intense problem of human suffering and I stressed that it is precisely through the Cross that the union of Christ with every man is achieved (n. 20).

Contemporary man has a remarkably clear perception of the drama of suffering and strongly feels the urgent need to ensure that a person is not left alone when faced with suffering. Much can be achieved in this regard by the solidarity of those who are moved by charity, especially when they can convey the good news of the redemption of suffering, through the Passion of Jesus.

161. The Congregation of the Passionists, which from the beginning has dedicated all its efforts to the field of evangelization, is now called to work with renewed vigor in the service of the new evangelization: the mystery of the Cross must be the focal point of all your efforts in this regard. The sons of Saint Paul of the Cross are heirs to a long tradition of catechesis and Gospel proclamation through popular missions, spiri-

tual exercises, spiritual direction and all those means which the love of the "most ingenious" God (*Rules,* 1775, c. 16) can devise. It is important to persevere in this work by renewing traditional forms and preparing new ones in harmony with your Founder's zeal.

I am also pleased with the numerous missions that the Congregation has undertaken in countries that are particularly in need of evangelization, carrying out a project which Saint Paul of the Cross always cherished. In the inevitable difficulties which these tasks involve, I urge all members to be steadfast in their conviction that God is preparing a great Christian and missionary springtime, the beginnings of which can already be seen (cf. *Redemptoris missio* n. 86). It is essential that they never forget that the Cross is the distinctive sign identifying Christianity as such and distinguishing it from every other religion. In the present age, when confusion often creeps into many souls particularly through the spread of sects and esoteric cults, the Passionists are called to emphasize *the distinctive and irreplaceable nature of the kerygma of the Cross,* an essential element of the proclamation of salvation.

162. Saint Paul of the Cross communicated the "charism" of the Passion first to his "companions," whom from his early youth he felt inspired to gather around him, and then, through them to the whole Congregation and the other Institutes and Movements related to it. The Church has recognized the authenticity of this charism, entrusting the Congregation with the specific task of keeping the "*memoria Passionis*" ever alive, fostering it both in spiritual, personal and community searching and in the apostolate addressed directly to the people. Indeed, it is vitally important to work so that the Cross of Christ is not emptied of its meaning (cf. 1 Cor 1:17), being vigilant so as to unmask the deceit with which the world tends

to appropriate God's own gifts and to distort the image of Christ impressed on believers through baptism.

163. This discernment requires deep detachment from worldly things and authentic poverty of spirit, virtues which were extremely dear to your Founder, who, in this regard, spoke of mystical death in order to be reborn in God, inviting us to immerse ourselves in our own "nothingness": to have no power, no possessions, no knowledge.

Faithful to the tradition that they should be masters of prayer (cf. *Consti.*, 37), the Passionists will continue to cultivate a strong spirituality that communicates to the many other souls thirsting for perfection a desire to participate in the self-abasement of Christ, in order to be reborn every day to a higher life (cf. *Redemptionis donum,* n. 10). This presupposes attentive listening to God, a task that Saint Paul of the Cross, in his spiritual testament, meant to safeguard and preserve through poverty, solitude and prayer. It is precisely by listening to God that we can listen to man, to his suffering, to his hunger for God and for justice.

164. Today, the Passion of Jesus and human suffering form one of the most timely themes of theology and ethics. On this topic it is easier to find a basis for dialogue both with Christians of other confessions and with other believers in God and, in general, with all people who are motivated by a sincere search for justice and love. Among the sons of Saint Paul of the Cross there have been some authentic forerunners of the ecumenical movement, enthusiastic apostles of the unity of all Christians, such as Blessed Dominic Barberi and Father Ignatius Spencer. They felt they were the heirs to the longing for unity characteristic of the Founder himself, who prayed intensely for this objective.

165.   Today's Passionists must not be anything less, but should continue to point to Christ crucified as the One who through his sacrifice broke down the dividing wall and reconciled every man to God and to his own brothers and sisters (cf. Eph 2:14-16). Like the Apostle, they must be deeply enthusiastic about Christ's Cross, folly for the world today, but the most profound wisdom for those who seek God, justice and peace.

I entrust the initiatives which the Congregation intends to carry out for the third centenary of their Founder's birth to Mary most holy and, through her maternal intercession, I invoke for every Passionist the commitment to and joy of being a credible witness to the Cross of Christ.

With these sentiments, I impart a special apostolic blessing to you, to the men and women religious of the Congregation of the Passion and to all the members of the Institutes and Movements who identify with the charism of Saint Paul of the Cross.

24

HOMILY FOR THE OPENING MASS OF THE SYNOD OF BISHOPS ON THE CONSECRATED LIFE

October 2, 1994

166.   "Follow me!" (Mk 10:21). Today we return again to this evocative Gospel passage: Christ's dialogue with the young man. It is *a simple yet extraordinarily rich text*, which offers a wealth of subjects for further reflection. In my *Letter to the Youth of the World* for Youth Year in 1985, I already commented on it at length. And the most recent Encyclical *Veritatis splendor* also refers to this Gospel text (cf. nn. 6-22).

Today, *as we open the Synod of Bishops dedicated to the consecrated life* and to the role of religious Institutes in the Church, once again *Christ's invitation* echoes in our ears. Each of us, venerable and dear brothers and sisters, has heard this call "Follow me!" at a certain point in life, an invitation with an inner force of its own: the grace of a vocation. The strength came from him who was speaking. The Good Teacher spoke through the Holy Spirit: the Spirit of truth, the Spirit of vocations.

167.   *For some time we have been preparing* this Synod on the theme: "The Consecrated Life and its Role in the Church and in the World." This topic reminds us that religious communities are called to the duty of perfection, clearly expressed by Christ in his conversation with the young man: "If you wish to be perfect" (Mt 19:21).

Later, down the centuries, the Church's tradition has given a doctrinal and practical expression to these words. The state of perfection is not only theory. It is life. And it is precisely life that confirms the truth of Christ's words: do not the majority of canonized saints come from religious Orders or Congregations?

It could be said that *the horizon of God's Kingdom* was disclosed and is constantly disclosed in a unique way through the vocation to the consecrated life. Does not the marvelous flourishing of secular Institutes and *Societies of apostolic life,* which are doing such good in the Church, date from the present time? We are also witnessing the birth of new forms of consecration, particularly within Church movements and associations, which seek to express, in ways appropriate to our contemporary culture, the traditional striving of religious life to contemplate the mystery of God and to fulfill a mission to our brothers and sisters.

168.   Hence, the Synod on religious life cannot fail to have particular importance for all the Church's members, who will be sure to support its work with their prayer.

It is significant that, after the recent Council, as Synods were held on various aspects of the conciliar teaching on the Church, only now have we come to one dedicated to religious Institutes, in other words, after the Synods on the Christian family (1980: *Familiaris consortio*), on the life of the laity (1987:*Christifideles laici*), on the ministry of priests in the Church (1990: *Pastores dabo vobis*).

One could almost say that *the journey we had to make* from the Second Vatican Council to this theme was greater. Work on it developed more slowly in the Church and in theological reflection. And now — we keenly hope — has come the suitable moment to address it: *the "kairos"* has come, the providential opportunity offered us by the Lord in order to make a thorough examination of the themes and perspectives already found in the conciliar texts. The members of religious

Communities and Institutes of consecrated life, inspired by the model of the early Church (Acts 2:42), should commit themselves with renewed zeal to being of one heart and soul, nourished by the Gospel teachings, the sacred liturgy and especially by the Eucharist, and persevering in prayer and in the communion of the same Spirit (cf. *Perfectae caritatis,* n. 15).

"Go, sell what you have and give to the poor and you will have treasure in heaven" (Mk 10:21). If we read attentively the text of today's liturgy, especially the Gospel passage, we can reach a conclusion: that in a certain sense, they contain the content of the first draft of the *Instrumentum laboris* of this Synod Assembly. Christ's dialogue with the young man highlights the meaning and value of Gospel *poverty*. It also sheds light on the question of *"renouncing marriage for the Kingdom of heaven,"* mentioned in Saint Matthew's Gospel (cf. 19:12), and enables us to understand the meaning of that *obedience* that makes a person like him who "obediently accepted even death" (Phil 2:8).

169.   *"We have given up everything and followed you"* (Mk 10:28), Peter said. These are words which the Church applies to you in particular, dear brothers and sisters.

Although the dialogue with the young man, as well as Peter's words, seem to refer only to men, nevertheless the ancient tradition of the *"bride"* and of *"spousal love"* should not be forgotten (cf. Hos 2:16-25; Ps 44 [45]:11-18; Rev 21:1-27). How many women down the centuries and generations have discovered their "role" in a contemplative or apostolic religious vocation, beginning with her who, as the *All Holy*, became in a certain sense the Church's "type," or model. The Synod's theme should therefore be read in the light of chapter eight of *Lumen gentium*. It should also take into account all I sought to express in *Mulieris dignitatem,* published in 1988, on the occasion of the Marian Year.

170. "Indeed, the word of God is living and effective, sharper than any two-edged sword ..., able to discern the reflections and thoughts of the heart" (Heb 4:12).

Such is the word of the living God. *The Synod's work must show that it particularly shares* in it.

From the very first day we are praying that everything the Synod says will be "effective," that is, able "to discern the reflections and thoughts of the heart."

We pray that this will occur throughout our Synod Assembly; we pray *for the bishops,* who together with the Bishop of Rome "canonically" have the leading role in the Synod. We also invoke the Holy Spirit for those in this Assembly who *directly represent the consecrated life,* male and female, that they may experience *a particular sharing of their own in that "word of God"* which is *"living."*

And what does it mean that it is also "sharper than any two-edged sword?" Love always lives by truth.

"Teach us to number our days aright, that we may gain wisdom of heart" (Ps 89 [90]:12).

Thus the Psalmist prayed. And his words are in step with the first reading: "Therefore I prayed, and prudence was given me; I pleaded and *the spirit of wisdom came to me....* Yet all good things together came to me in her company, and countless riches at her hands" (Wis 7:7, 11).

Yes, venerable and beloved brothers and sisters. *The Synod is your vocation for this month.* It is a great good for the whole People of God, a particular treasure for all the Church's members.

171. And how could we not recall that the Synod dedicated to consecrated life in the Church is taking place during the *"Year of the Family?"* In a week's time, families will gather here in Rome from every corner of the earth, to "celebrate" solemnly their

presence and mission in the Church. The Council speaks of the vocation of married couples as a specific "consecration."

Is there not something providential in this coincidence? Does it not offer us the opportunity for a deeper understanding of the mystery of the religious consecration, which is the providential "wealth and riches" of the Church? The Lord wants to lead us to discover with the eyes of faith *how these two vocations mutually complement each other, so that we will praise God* for the variety of his gifts. Just as with the words of the "Magnificat" the Lord was praised by *Mary,* a human being who in herself admirably combined the vocation of virginal Spouse of the Holy Spirit and Mother of the Holy Family.

"God who is mighty has done great things for me, holy is his name" (Lk 1:49). Amen!

25

HOMILY FOR THE CLOSING MASS
OF THE SYNOD OF BISHOPS
ON THE CONSECRATED LIFE

October 29, 1994

172. *"Quia fecit mihi magna."* "For he who is mighty has done great things for me" (Lk 1:49).

With this celebration we conclude the work of the Ninth Ordinary General Assembly of the Synod of Bishops, dedicated to consecrated life and its role in the Church and in the world. We close it on a Saturday — a day traditionally *dedicated to the Mother of God.* Thus in today's Eucharistic sacrifice we turn particularly to Mary, borrowing the words of thanksgiving from the *Magnificat,* which the Church repeats every day in the Liturgy of the Hours: *"He has done great things for me,"* "Fecit mihi magna qui potens est."

173. The *Second Vatican Council* was a "great thing" for the Church and could rightly be called the most significant ecclesial event of our century. Against the background of this first, fundamental "great thing" given to us by the Lord, other "great things" can be recognized that were achieved by him in the recent past. Among these is surely the institution of the *Synod of Bishops,* which by now has developed its own history during the post-conciliar period. This most recent Synod Assembly can now be added to the list; it was long awaited and — we hope — no less fruitful than its predecessors.

We will thus have the joy of following the Apostolic Exhortations *Familiaris consortio, Christifideles laici* and *Pastores dabo vobis* with a new *post-synodal document,* whose *incipit* we do not know yet, but which will certainly reflect what emerged during the Assembly that closes today. They were certainly weeks of intense work, during which consecrated life and its role have been the focus of the Church's reflection and prayer.

174.   *My soul thirsts for God, the living God* (Ps 41 [42]:3).
       The readings just proclaimed shed great light on the unique state of ecclesial life that is consecrated life. The responsorial psalm *recalls the liturgy of Baptism*, with the blessing of holy water during the great Easter Vigil of Holy Saturday.
       Baptism is *the human person's first and fundamental consecration*. Beginning a new life in Christ, a baptized man or woman shares in that consecration, that total self-giving to the Father which is proper to his eternal Son. It is he himself—the Son—who *stirs up in the human soul the desire to give oneself unreservedly to God:* "My soul thirsts for God, the living God. When shall I come and behold the face of God?" (Ps 41 [42]:3).

175.   Religious consecration, with its distinct *eschatological dimension*, is grafted onto baptismal consecration. No one has ever seen God (cf. Jn 1:18) in this life. Nevertheless, the beatific vision, that is, seeing God "face to face" (1 Cor 13:12), is the definitive vocation, beyond time, of every human being. Consecrated persons have the task of reminding everyone of this. *Faith prepares us for this beatific vision, in which God gives himself to man* in the measure of love in which the latter has responded to the eternal Love revealed in the Incarnation and Cross of Christ.

176.   *"For to me to live is Christ"* (Phil 1:21), writes the apostle Paul.
       "Amori Christi nihil praeponatur" (to prefer nothing to the love of Christ)—*Saint Benedict* proclaims in his
170

Rule. "Amori Christi in pauperibus nihil praeponatur" (to prefer nothing to the love of Christ in the poor). *Saint Vincent de Paul* will say a thousand years later.

What marvelous power these words contain! Are European culture and civilization conceivable without them? Can the great missionary epics of the first and second millennia be imagined without them? And what could be said of Eastern Christian monasticism, whose origins go back to the first centuries of Christianity? See, those who left the world to follow the poor, chaste and obedient Christ at the same time transformed it. In them was fulfilled the entreaty: "Send forth your Spirit and renew the face of the earth" (cf. Ps 103 [104]:30). The Holy Spirit knows the "times and moments" when people suited to the tasks required by historical circumstances must be called upon.

In his time, he called Benedict and his sister Scholastica. He called Bernard, Francis and Clare of Assisi, Bonaventure, Dominic, Thomas Aquinas and Saint Catherine of Siena. The Gospel went from public squares to university chairs. At the time of the *Western schism and the Reformation,* he called Ignatius of Loyola, Teresa of Avila, John of the Cross, and then Francis Xavier and Peter Claver. Through them a profound spiritual reform was achieved and the missionary epic began in the East and West.

177. *In the centuries closest to us,* the Spirit who renews the face of the earth called others such as John Baptist de la Salle, Paul of the Cross, Alphonsus Mary de' Liguori and John Bosco, to mention only a few of the better-known. *At the end of the last century and throughout the present,* the same Spirit of the Father and the Son spoke through Thérèse of the Child Jesus, Maximilian Kolbe and Sister Faustina.

What would the ancient and modern world be without these figures — and those of many others? They learned from Christ that *"his yoke is easy and his burden light"* (cf. Mt 11:30) — and *they taught it to others.*

178. We conclude this Synod Assembly almost *on the eve of the Solemnity of All Saints.* The Book of Revelation speaks of this immense throng from every nation and race, people and tongue, standing before the heavenly throne and the Lamb of God (cf. 7:9). The significant question follows: *"Who are these, clothed in white robes, and whence have they come?"*

From where have they come? — we too wonder. *Do they not come from the countless Institutes of consecrated life,* for men and women, present in the Church? The canonizations and beatifications proclaimed down the centuries attest to this. The beatifications that have taken place this month during the Synod particularly attest to this.

179. Today, the last Saturday of October, we offer to you, Mary, *Mother and Virgin, the humble handmaid of the Lord and Queen of all saints,* the fruits of this Synod's work. We entrust them to you, Queen of the holy Rosary, Queen of this beautiful prayer which has sustained us day by day throughout the month.

Grant that these fruits, by a unique exchange of gifts, may also help *the cause of the Family* and fulfill the plan of divine Providence, which wanted the Synod on consecrated life to be celebrated during the Year of the Family.

Consecrated persons praise you, Lord.

The Christian families of the whole world praise you.

The Church praises you for the gift of the Synod.

"Magnificat anima mea Dominum" (Lk 1:46).

JOHN PAUL II

CATECHESES ON
"THE CONSECRATED LIFE"

GIVEN DURING THE WEDNESDAY
GENERAL AUDIENCES

First series: September-December 1994

---

* A second series of catecheses on the consecrated life was given in 1995. The life of prayer and the apostolate are emphasized in this series.

26

"THE CONSECRATED LIFE,
A DIVINE GIFT IN THE CHURCH"

September 28, 1994

180. In the ecclesiological catecheses we have been giving for some time, we have often presented the Church as a "priestly" people, i.e., comprising persons who share in Christ's priesthood as a state of consecration to God and of offering the perfect, definitive worship he gives to the Father in the name of all humanity. This is a result of baptism, which inserts the believer into Christ's Mystical Body and appoints him — almost *ex officio* and, one could say, in an institutional way — to reproduce in himself the condition of Priest and Victim (*Sacerdos et Hostia)* of the Head (cf. Saint Thomas, *Summa Theol.*, III, q. 63, a. 3 in c. and ad 2; a. 6).

Every other sacrament — especially confirmation — completes this spiritual state of the believer, and the sacrament of Orders also confers the power to act ministerially as Christ's instrument in proclaiming the Word, renewing the sacrifice of the Cross and forgiving sin.

181. To explain better this consecration of the People of God, we now would like to discuss another basic chapter of ecclesiology, which in our day has become increasingly important from the theological and spiritual standpoint. We are speaking of *the consecrated life*, which many of Christ's followers embrace as a particularly elevated, intense and demanding way of living out the consequences of baptism with a lofty charity leading to perfection and holiness.

The Second Vatican Council, heir to the theological and spiritual tradition of two millennia of Christianity, has highlighted the value of the consecrated life, which — according to what the Gospel indicates — "is expressed in the practice of *chastity* consecrated to God, *poverty* and *obedience,*" which are called precisely the "evangelical counsels" (cf. Constitution *Lumen gentium,* n. 43). The Council speaks of them as a spontaneous manifestation of the sovereign action of the Holy Spirit, who from the beginning has produced an abundance of generous souls moved by the desire for perfection and self-giving for the good of all Christ's body (cf. *Lumen gentium,* n. 43).

182.   We are speaking of individual experiences, which have never been lacking and even today continue to blossom in the Church. However, since the first centuries a tendency has been noted to move from the personal and — one could almost say — "private" practice of the evangelical counsels to a state of *public recognition by the Church*, both in the solitary life of *hermits* and — ever increasingly — in the formation of *monastic communities* or *religious families*, which are meant to assist in attaining the objectives of the *consecrated life:* stability, better doctrinal formation, obedience, mutual help and progress in charity.

Thus, from the first centuries down to our day, "a wondrous variety of religious communities" has emerged, in which the "manifold wisdom of God" is displayed (cf. Decree *Perfectae caritatis,* n. 1) and the Church's extraordinary vitality is expressed, but in the unity of Christ's Body, according to the words of Saint Paul: "There are different gifts but the same Spirit" (1 Cor. 12:4). The Spirit pours out his gifts in a great variety of forms to enrich the one Church, which in her multicolored beauty reveals in time "the unfathomable riches of Christ" (Eph 3:8), as all creation manifests "in many forms and in each individual part" (*multipliciter et divisim*), as Saint Thomas says (*Summa Theol.*, I, q. 47, a. 1), what in God is absolute unity.

183. In every case, it is a question of one basic "divine gift," although in the multiplicity and variety of spiritual gifts or charisms bestowed on individuals and communities (cf. *Summa Theol.*, II-II, q. 103, a. 2). Charisms in fact can be individual or collective. The individual ones are widespread in the Church and vary so much from person to person that they are difficult to categorize and in each case require the Church's discernment. Collective charisms are generally bestowed on men and women who are destined to establish ecclesial works, especially religious Institutes, which receive their distinctive mark from their founders' charisms, live and work under their influence and, to the extent of their fidelity, receive new gifts and charisms for each individual member and for the community as a whole. The latter can thus discover new forms of activity in accordance with the needs of time and place, without breaking the line of continuity and development going back to the founder, or by easily recovering its identity and vigor.

184. The Council observes that "the Church, by virtue of her authority, gladly accepted and approved" religious families (*Perfectae caritatis*, n. 1). This was in harmony with her own responsibility for charisms, because it is her "office not indeed to extinguish the Spirit, but to test all things and hold fast to what is good (cf. 1 Thes 5:12, 19-21; *Lumen gentium*, n. 2). This explains why — with regard to the evangelical counsels — "the authority of the Church, under the guidance of the Holy Spirit, has taken on the task of interpreting these counsels and regulating their practice as well as establishing stable forms of living according to them" (*Lumen gentium*, n. 43).

185. It should always be kept in mind, however, that the state of consecrated life does not belong to the hierarchical structure of the Church. The Council notes this: "If one considers the divine and hierarchical constitution of the Church, the religious state is not an intermediate condition between the clerical and lay. But some faithful, from each of these two conditions (clerical and lay), are called by God to enjoy a particular gift in the life of the Church and, each in their own way, to help the Church in her mission of salvation" (*Lumen gentium,* n. 43).

The Council immediately adds, however, that the religious state, "which is constituted by the profession of the evangelical counsels, although it does not belong to the hierarchical structure of the Church, does, however, belong *unquestionably* to her life and holiness" (*Lumen gentium,* n. 44). This adverb — "unquestionably" — means that all the blows that can disturb the Church's life will never be able to eliminate the consecrated life characterized by the profession of the evangelical counsels. This state of life will endure as an essential element of the Church's holiness. According to the Council, this is an "unshakable" truth.

186. That having been said, it must still be stated clearly that no particular form of consecrated life is sure to last forever. Individual religious communities can die out. History shows that some have in fact disappeared, just as certain "particular" Churches have also come to an end. Institutes that are no longer suited to their age, or which have no more vocations, can be forced to close or to be consolidated with others. The guarantee of lasting until the end of the world, which was given to the Church as a whole, has not necessarily been granted to individual religious Institutes. History teaches that the charism of the consecrated life is always

on the move, showing that it can discover and *invent*, so to speak, new forms that more directly answer the needs and aspirations of the time, while remaining faithful to the founder's charism. However, communities that have existed for centuries are also called to adapt to these needs and aspirations so as not to condemn themselves to disappearing.

187.   Nevertheless, the practice of the evangelical counsels — whatever forms it may take — is guaranteed to last throughout history, because Jesus Christ himself desired and established it as a definitive feature of the Church's economy of holiness. The idea of a Church consisting only of lay people involved in marriage and secular professions does not correspond to Christ's intentions as we find them in the Gospel. All this shows us — from also looking at history and even current events — that there will always be men and women (and boys and girls) who will want to give themselves totally to Christ and his Kingdom by the way of celibacy, poverty and submission to a rule of life. Those who take this way will continue, in the future as in the past, to play an important role for the Christian community's growth in holiness and for its evangelizing mission. Indeed, today more than ever, the way of the evangelical counsels offers great hope for the future of the Church.

27

"RECENT DEVELOPMENTS AND ORIENTATIONS OF THE CONSECRATED LIFE"

October 5, 1994

188.   Consecrated life, which has marked the Church's development over the centuries, has experienced and still experiences different expressions. This variety must be kept in mind while reading the chapter of the Constitution *Lumen gentium* dedicated to the profession of the evangelical counsels. It bears the title "Religious," but the range of its doctrinal considerations and pastoral intentions covers the much wider and diversified area of consecrated life as it has developed in recent years.

Many people today also choose the way of consecrated life in religious Institutes and Congregations that have long been active in the Church, which continues to find new enrichment in the spiritual life from their living, fruitful presence.

189.   In the Church today, however, there are also new visible associations of consecrated persons, recognized and regulated from the canonical standpoint. First of all, there are the *secular Institutes,* in which, according to the *Code of Canon Law,* "the Christian faithful living in the world strive for the perfection of charity and work for the sanctification of the world especially from within" (can. 710). The members of these Institutes are obliged to follow the evangelical counsels, but they harmonize them with a life of involvement in the world of secular activity and institutions. For many years, even before the Council, there were some gifted pioneers in this form of consecrated life, which —

externally — is more like that of "seculars" than of "religious." For some this choice was perhaps based on necessity, in that they were not able to enter a religious community because of certain family obligations or certain obstacles. But for many it was the commitment to an ideal: to combine an authentic consecration to God with a life lived amid the affairs of the world, and this too as a vocation. It is to Pope Pius XII's credit to have recognized the legitimacy of this form of consecration in the Apostolic Constitution *Provida Mater Ecclesia* (1947).

190. In addition to secular Institutes, the *Code of Canon Law* recognizes *Societies of apostolic life,* "whose members without religious vows pursue the particular apostolic purpose of the society, and leading a life as brothers or sisters in common according to a particular manner of life, strive for the perfection of charity through the observance of the constitutions" (can. 731). Among these societies, which are "assimilated" to the Institutes of consecrated life, there are some whose members are committed to practicing the evangelical counsels by a bond defined in the Constitutions. This too is a form of consecration.

191. In more recent times, a certain number of "movements" or "ecclesial associations" have appeared. I spoke of them appreciatively on the occasion of a convention sponsored by the Italian Episcopal Conference on *The Christian Community and Associations of the Laity:* "The phenomenon of ecclesial associations," I said, "is a fact characterizing the present historical moment of the Church. And it must also be noted, with true consolation, that the range of these associations covers the entire span of the forms of the Christian's presence in current society" (*Insegnamenti,* VII, 2, 1984, 290; *L'Osservatore Romano* English edition, Sept. 17,

1984, p. 8). Now as then, I hope that, in order to avoid the risk of a certain self-satisfaction on the part of those who tend to absolutize their own experience, and of an isolation from the community life of the local Churches and their pastors, these lay associations will live "in full ecclesial communion with the bishop" (*ibid.*, p. 292).

192.   These "movements" or "associations," although consisting of lay people, often steer their members — or some of their members — towards practicing the evangelical counsels. Consequently, even if they are defined as lay people, groups or communities of consecrated life arise among them. What is more, this form of consecrated life can be accompanied by an openness to the priestly ministry, when some communities accept priests or guide young men to priestly ordination. As a result, some of these movements reflect the image of the Church according to the three directions that the development of her historical composition can take: those of *lay people,* of *priests* and of *consecrated souls* within the context of the evangelical counsels.

193.   One need only refer to this new situation without having to describe the various movements in detail, in order to emphasize the significance of their presence in the Church today.

It is important to see them as a sign of the charisms given to the Church by the Holy Spirit in ever new and at times unforeseeable ways. The experience of recent years allows us to state that, in harmony with the foundations of the faith, the charismatic life is far from being spent, but is finding new expressions in the Church, especially in the forms of consecrated life.

194.   A very particular — and in a certain sense, new — aspect of this experience is the importance that

the lay character generally has in it. It is true that there can be some misunderstandings about the word "lay," even in the religious sphere. When lay people are committed to the way of the evangelical counsels, doubtless they belong to a certain extent to a state of consecrated life that is very different from what is more commonly that of other believers who choose marriage and secular professions. "Consecrated" lay people, however, intend to maintain and strengthen their attachment to the title "lay," since they wish to be and to be known as members of the People of God, in accordance with the origin of the word "lay" (from *laós:* people), and to give witness to the fact that they belong to this people, without distancing themselves from their brothers and sisters even in civil life.

195.   Also of considerable importance and interest is the ecclesial vision of movements which show a firm intention to live the life of the whole Church, as a community of Christ's followers, and to reflect it in deep union and collaboration between "lay people," religious and priests in their personal decisions and in the apostolate.

It is true that these three characteristics, i.e., charismatic vitality, the desire to give witness to one's membership in the People of God and the requirement of communion for consecrated persons with lay people and priests, are features common to all forms of consecrated religious life; but we must acknowledge that they are expressed more intensely in contemporary movements, which are generally distinguished by a deep commitment of dedication to the mystery of the Church and of skilled service to her mission.

196.   In addition to movements and communities of a "lay-ecclesial" orientation, we must now mention other types of recent communities, which put greater

stress on the traditional elements of religious life. Some of these new communities have a strictly monastic orientation, with a notable development of liturgical prayer; others follow in the "canon" tradition, which along with the more strictly "monastic" tradition, was so active in the Middle Ages, having particular care for parishes and, later, for a more extensive apostolate. Even more radical today is the new "eremitical" tendency, with the foundation or rebirth of both old- and new-style hermitages.

197.   On a superficial glance, some of these forms of consecrated life could seem out of step with the current direction of ecclesial life. In fact, however, the Church — which certainly needs consecrated persons who turn more directly to the world in order to evangelize it — also needs, and perhaps even more so, those who seek, cultivate and give witness to God's presence and intimacy, with the intention of working for the sanctification of the world. These are the two aspects of consecrated life seen in Jesus Christ, who reached out to men to bring them light and life, but also sought solitude to devote himself to prayer and contemplation. Neither of these two requirements can be neglected in the Church's life today. We must be grateful to the Holy Spirit who enables us to understand this continually through the charisms he abundantly distributes and the often surprising initiatives he inspires.

28

"ACCORDING TO
THE FOUNDING WILL OF CHRIST"

October 12, 1994

198.   What counts the most in the old and new forms of "consecrated life" is that one perceives in them a basic conformity with the will of Christ, who instituted the evangelical counsels and is, in this sense, the founder of religious life and of every similar state of consecration. As the Second Vatican Council said, the evangelical counsels are "based on the teaching and example of Christ" (*Lumen gentium,* n. 43).

Some have doubted this basis by considering the consecrated life as a purely human institution that arose from the initiative of Christians who wanted to live the Gospel ideal more deeply. Now, it is true that Jesus did not directly found any of the religious communities that gradually grew up in the Church, nor did he determine the particular forms of consecrated life. However, what he wanted and established is the state of consecrated life in its overall value and essential elements. There is no historical evidence that can explain this state as a later human initiative, nor can one readily conceive that consecrated life — which has played so large a role in the growth of the Church's holiness and mission — did not stem from the founding will of Christ. If we carefully explore the Gospel testimonies, we will discover that this will can be seen very clearly.

199.   The Gospel shows that from the beginning of his public life Jesus called men to follow him. This call was not necessarily expressed in words: it could result merely from the attraction Jesus' personality held for

those he met, as in the case of the first two disciples according to the account of John's Gospel. Already disciples of John the Baptist, Andrew and his companion (who seems to have been the evangelist himself) were fascinated and almost carried away by the one presented to them as "the Lamb of God;" they immediately began to follow Jesus, even before he had said a word to them. When Jesus asked: "What are you looking for?," they answered with another question: "Teacher, where do you stay?" Then they received the invitation that would change their lives: "Come and see" (cf. Jn 1:38-39).

200.   In general, however, the most characteristic expression of the call are the words: "Follow me" (Mt 8:22; 9:9; 19:21; Mk 2:14; 10:21; Lk 9:59; 18:22; Jn 1:43; 21:19). It shows Jesus' initiative. Before that time, those who wanted to embrace a master's teaching chose the person whose pupils they wished to become. With the words: "Follow me," however, Jesus shows that he is the one who chooses the companions and disciples he wishes to have. In fact, he will say to the apostles: "It was not you who chose me, it was I who chose you" (Jn 15:16).

In Jesus' initiative, a sovereign will appears, but also intense love. The account of the call addressed to the rich young man reveals this love. There we read that, when the rich young man stated that he had observed the commandments of the law since his childhood, Jesus "looked at him with love" (Mk 10:21). This penetrating, loving gaze accompanied the invitation: "Go and sell what you have and give to the poor; you will then have treasure in heaven. After that, come and follow me" (ibid.). Jesus' divine and human love, so burning as to be recalled by a witness to the scene, is repeated in every call to total self-giving in the consecrated life. As I wrote in the Apostolic Exhortation Redemptionis donum: "This love reflects *the eternal love of the Father,* who 'so loved the world that he gave his only Son, that whoever believes in him should not perish but have eternal life' (Jn 3:16)" (n. 3).

201. The Gospel also attests that the call to follow Jesus makes many broad demands: the account of the invitation to the rich young man stresses the renunciation of material possessions; in other cases the renunciation of one's family is more expressly emphasized (cf. for example, Lk 9:59-60). In general, following Jesus means renouncing everything in order to be united with him and to accompany him on the paths of his mission. This is the renunciation to which the apostles agreed, when Peter declared: "Here we have put everything aside to follow you" (Mt 19:27). Precisely in his response to Peter, Jesus indicates the renunciation of human possessions as the basic component in following him (cf. Mt 19:29). The Old Testament shows that God asked his people to follow him by observing the commandments, but without ever making such radical demands. Jesus reveals his divine sovereignty, on the other hand, by requiring absolute devotion to himself, to the point of total detachment from earthly possessions and affections.

202. It should be noted, however, that although he made new demands in the call to follow him, Jesus offers them for the free choice of those he calls. They are not precepts, but invitations or "counsels." The love with which Jesus addressed the call did not take away the rich young man's power to decide freely, as shown by his refusal to follow Jesus because he preferred his possessions. The evangelist Mark notes that he "went away sad, for he had many possessions" (Mk 10:22). Jesus did not condemn him for this. But he remarked in turn, and not without some sadness, that it is difficult for the rich to

enter the Kingdom of heaven and that only God can bring about certain detachments, a certain interior freedom that makes it possible to answer the call (cf. Mk 10:23-27).

203. On the other hand, Jesus promises that the renunciations required by the call to follow him will receive their recompense, "treasure in heaven," that is, an abundance of spiritual goods. He even promises eternal life in the world to come and a hundredfold in this present age (cf. Mt 19:29). This hundredfold refers to a higher quality of life, a superior happiness. Experience teaches that consecrated life, according to Jesus' plan, is a deeply happy life. This happiness is measured according to fidelity to Jesus' plan. This is true even though, as the reference to persecution recorded by Mark in the same episode (10:30) suggests, the "hundredfold" does not spare one from sharing in Christ's Cross.

204. Jesus also called women to follow him. A Gospel witness says that a group of women accompanied Jesus and these women were many (cf. Lk 8:1-3; Mt 27:55; Mk 15:40-41). This was a great novelty with respect to Jewish custom: only Jesus' innovative will, which included the advancement and, in a certain way, the liberation of women, can explain this fact. No Gospel account of the call of any woman has come down to us. However, the presence of many women with the Twelve around Jesus presupposes a call on his part, a choice whether silent or expressed.

205. Jesus in fact shows that the state of consecrated life which consists in following him is not necessarily connected with the goal of priestly ministry, and that this state includes both women and men, each in his

or her own area and with the role determined by the divine call. In the group of women following Jesus we can see a sign and even the initial nucleus of the enormous number of women who will be dedicated to religious life or other forms of consecrated life over the Church's centuries down to our day. This applies to "consecrated" women but also to so many other sisters of ours who in new ways follow the authentic example of Jesus' collaborators: for example, as lay "volunteers" in many apostolic tasks and in many offices and ministries of the Church.

206.   We conclude this catechesis by recognizing that, in calling men and women to abandon everything in order to follow him, Jesus inaugurated a state of life which would gradually develop in the Church in the various forms of consecrated life expressed in religious life, or also — for those chosen by God — in the priesthood. From Gospel times to our own day, Christ's founding will has continued to be at work, the will expressed in that very beautiful and holy invitation addressed to so many souls: "Follow me!"

29

"HOW TO FOSTER VOCATIONS TO THE CONSECRATED LIFE"

October 19, 1994

207. In discussing the foundation of consecrated life on the part of Jesus Christ, we mentioned the calls he extended from the beginning of his public life, generally expressed in the words: "Follow me." Jesus' care in making these appeals shows the importance he attributed to Gospel discipleship for the life of the Church. He linked that discipleship with the "counsels" of consecrated life, which he desired for his disciples as that conformation to himself which is the heart of Gospel holiness (cf. *Veritatis splendor*, n. 21). In fact, history confirms that consecrated persons — priests, men and women religious, members of other Institutes and similar movements — have played an essential role in the Church's expansion, as they have in her growth in holiness and love.

In the Church today, vocations to religious life have no less importance than in centuries past. Unfortunately, in many places we see that their number is insufficient for meeting the needs of communities and their apostolate. It is no exaggeration to say that for some Institutes this problem has become critical, to the point of threatening their survival. Even without wishing to share the dire predictions for the not-too-distant future, it is already apparent today that, for lack of members, some communities are forced to give up works usually destined to produce abundant spiritual fruit and that, more generally, fewer vocations lead to a decline in the Church's active presence in society, with considerable losses in every field.

208. The present vocations shortage in some parts of the world is a challenge to be met with determination and courage, in the certainty that Jesus Christ, who during his earthly life called many to consecrated life, is still doing so in today's world and often receives a generous, positive response, as daily experience proves. Knowing the Church's needs, he continues to extend the invitation, "Follow me," particularly to young people, whom his grace makes responsive to the ideal of a life of total dedication.

In addition, the lack of workers for God's harvest was already a challenge in Gospel times for Jesus himself. His example teaches us that the shortage of consecrated persons is a situation inherent in the world's condition and not only an accidental fact due to contemporary circumstances. The Gospel tells us that as he roamed through towns and villages, Jesus was moved with pity for the crowds which "were lying prostrate from exhaustion, like sheep without a shepherd" (Mt 9:36). He tried to remedy that situation by teaching them at great length (cf. Mk 6:34), but he wanted the disciples to join him in solving the problem and so he invited them, first of all, to pray: "Beg the harvest Master to send out laborers to gather his harvest (Mt 9:38). According to the context, this prayer was intended to provide people with a greater number of *pastors*. However, the expression "laborers for the harvest" can have a wider application and indicate everyone who works for the Church's growth. The prayer, then, also seeks to obtain a greater number of *consecrated persons*.

209. The stress put on prayer is surprising. Given God's sovereign initiative in calling, we might think that only the harvest Master, independently of any other intervention or cooperation, should provide a sufficient number of workers. On the contrary, Jesus

insists on the cooperation and responsibility of his followers. He also teaches us today that with prayer we can and must influence the number of vocations. The Father welcomes this prayer because he wants it and expects it, and he himself makes it effective. Whenever and wherever the vocations crisis is more serious, this prayer is all the more necessary. But it must rise to heaven in every time and place. In this area the whole Church and every Christian always have a responsibility.

210.   This prayer must be joined to efforts to encourage an increase in the responses to the divine call. Here too we find the prime example in the Gospel. After his first contact with Jesus, Andrew brings his brother Simon to him (cf. Jn 1:42). Certainly, Jesus shows himself sovereign in his call to Simon, but on his own initiative Andrew played a decisive role in Simon's meeting with the Master. "In a way, this is the heart of all the Church's pastoral work on behalf of vocations" (cf. *Pastores dabo vobis,* n. 38).

211.   Encouraging vocations can come from personal initiative, like Andrew's, or from collective efforts, as is done in many dioceses that have developed a vocations apostolate. This promotion of vocations does not at all aim at restricting the individual's freedom of choice regarding the direction of his own life. This promotion, therefore, avoids putting any kind of constraint or pressure on each person's decision. But it seeks to shed light on everyone's choice and to show each individual, in particular, the way opened in his or her life by the Gospel's "Follow me." Young people especially need and have a right to receive this light. On the other hand, the seeds of a vocation, particularly in young people, must certainly be cultivated and strengthened. Vocations must develop and grow, which usually does not occur unless conditions favorable to this

development and growth are guaranteed. This is the purpose of institutions for vocations and the various programs, meetings, retreats, prayer groups, etc. that promote the work of vocations. One can never do enough in the vocations apostolate, even though every human initiative must always be based on the conviction that, in the end, each person's vocation depends on God's sovereign decision.

212.   A basic form of cooperation is the witness of consecrated persons themselves, which exercises a healthy, effective attraction. Experience shows that often the example of a man or woman religious has a decisive impact on the direction of a young personality which has been able to discover in their fidelity, integrity and joy the concrete example of an ideal way to live. In particular, religious communities can only attract young people by a collective witness of authentic consecration, lived in the joy of self-giving to Christ and to their brothers and sisters.

213.   Lastly, the importance of the family should be stressed as the Christian environment in which vocations can develop and grow. Once again I invite Christian parents to pray that Christ will call one of their children to the consecrated life. The task of Christian parents is to form a family in which Gospel values are honored, cultivated and lived, and where an authentic Christian life can elevate the aspirations of the young. It is because of these families that the Church will continue to produce vocations. Therefore, she asks families to collaborate in answering the "harvest Master," who wants us all to be committed to sending new "laborers into the harvest."

30

"NATURE AND DIMENSIONS OF THE CONSECRATION OF ONE'S LIFE BY THE EVANGELICAL COUNSELS"

October 26, 1994

214.   Several times in the preceding catecheses I have spoken of the "evangelical counsels," which in consecrated life are expressed as the "vows" — or at least commitments — of chastity, poverty and obedience. They find their full meaning in the context of a life *totally* dedicated to God in communion with Christ. The adverb "totally," used by Saint Thomas Aquinas to indicate the essential value of religious life, is most expressive! "Religion is a virtue whereby a man offers something to the service and worship of God. Therefore, those are called *religious* by antonomasia, who *consecrate themselves totally* to the divine service, as offering a *holocaust* to God" (*Summa Theol.*, II-II, q. 186, a.1). It is an idea drawn from the tradition of the Fathers, particularly from Saint Jerome (cf. *Epist.* 125, *ad Rusticum*), and from Saint Gregory the Great (cf. *Super Ezech.*, hom. 20). The Second Vatican Council, which quotes Saint Thomas Aquinas, made his teaching its own and speaks of a complete, interior "consecration to God" that, as a development of the baptismal consecration, takes place in the religious state through the bonds of the evangelical counsels (cf. *Lumen gentium*, n. 44).

215.   It should be noted that in this consecration human endeavor does not have priority. The initiaive comes from Christ, who asks for a freely accepted covenant in following him. It is he who, by taking possession of a human person, "consecrates" him.

According to the Old Testament, God himself consecrated persons or objects by imparting his holiness in some way to them. This should not be understood in the sense that God inwardly sanctified people, much less objects, but in the sense that he took possession of them and set them apart for his direct service. The "sacred" objects were intended for the worship of the Lord, and thus could only be used in the Temple and during worship, and not for what was *profane*. This *sacredness* was attributed to things that could not be touched by *profane* hands (for example, the Ark of the Covenant, the cups of the Temple in Jerusalem which were profaned — as we read in 1 Mc 1:22 — by Antiochus Epiphanes). In turn, the people of Israel were "holy" as the "Lord's possession" (*segullah* = the sovereign's personal treasury), and thus had a *sacred* character (cf. Ex 19:5; Dt 7:6; Ps 134[135]:4; etc.). To communicate with this "segullah," God chose "spokesmen," "men of God," "prophets," who were to speak in his name. He sanctified them (morally) through the relationship of trust and special friendship he reserved for them, so much so that some of these persons were called "God's friends" (cf. Wis 7:27; Is 41:8; Jas 2:23).

216.   However, there was no individual, means or institution that by its inner force could communicate God's holiness to men, however well-disposed. This would be the great newness of Christian baptism, by which believers have their "hearts sprinkled clean" (Heb 10:22), and are inwardly "washed, consecrated, justified in the name of our Lord Jesus Christ and in the Spirit of our God" (1 Cor 6:11).

The essential element of the Gospel law is grace, which is a power of life that justifies and saves, as Saint Thomas explains (cf. *Summa Theol.*, I-II, q. 106, a. 2), following Saint Augustine (cf. *De Spiritu et littera*, ch. 17). Christ already takes possession of the person from within through baptism, in which he begins his sanctifying action, "consecrating him" and instilling in him the need for a response that he himself makes possible by his grace, to the extent of the subject's physical, psychological, spiritual and moral capacity. The sovereign power exercised by the grace of Christ in consecration does not at all diminish the freedom of the response to the call, nor the value and importance of human effort. This is made particularly clear in the call to practice the evangelical counsels. Christ's call is accompanied by a grace that elevates the human person and gives him abilities of a higher order to follow these counsels. This means that in consecrated life there is a development of the human personality itself, which is not frustrated but elevated and enhanced by the divine gift.

217.   The person who accepts the call and follows the evangelical counsels performs a basic act of love for God, as we read in the Constitution *Lumen gentium* (n. 44) of the Second Vatican Council. The purpose of religious vows is to scale the heights of love: a complete love, dedicated to Christ under the impulse of the Holy Spirit and, through Christ, offered to the Father: hence the value of the oblation and consecration of religious profession, which in Eastern and Western Christian tradition is considered as a *baptismus flaminis,* (baptism in the Spirit), inasmuch as "a person's heart is moved by the Holy Spirit to believe in and love God, and to repent of his sins" (*Summa Theol.*, III, q. 66, a. 11).

    I explained this idea of an almost new baptism in the Letter *Redemptionis donum:* "Religious profession," I wrote, "is a new 'burial in the death of Christ': new, because it is made of love and vocation; new, by reason of unceasing 'conversion.' This 'burial in death' causes the person 'buried together with Christ' to *walk like Christ in newness of life.'* In Christ crucified is to be found the ultimate foundation both of baptismal consecration and of the profession of the evangelical counsels, which — in the words of the Second Vatican Council — 'constitutes a special consecration.' It is at one and the same time both *death and liberation*. Saint Paul writes: 'Consider yourselves dead to sin.' At the same time he calls this death 'freedom from the slavery of sin.' Above all, though, religious consecration, through its sacramental foundation in holy baptism, constitutes a new life 'for God in Jesus Christ'" (*Redemptionis donum,* n. 7).

218.   This life is all the more perfect and produces more abundant fruits of baptismal grace (cf. *Lumen gentium,* n. 44), inasmuch as the intimate union with Christ received in baptism develops into a more complete union. Indeed, the commandment to love God with all one's heart, which is enjoined on the baptized, is observed to the full by the love vowed to God through the evangelical counsels. It is a "special consecration" (*Perfectae caritatis,* n. 5); a closer consecration to the divine service "by a new and special title" *(Lumen gentium,* n. 44); a new consecration, which cannot be considered an implication or logical consequence of baptism. Baptism does not necessarily imply an orientation towards celibacy and the renunciation of material possessions in the form of the evangelical counsels. Religious consecration, instead, means the call to a new life that implies the gift of an original charism not granted to everyone, as Jesus states when he speaks of voluntary celibacy (cf. Mt 19:10-12). Hence, it is a sovereign act of God, who freely chooses, calls, opens a way that is certainly connected with the baptismal consecration, but is distinct from it.

219.   In a similar way, it can be said that the profession of the evangelical counsels further develops the consecration received in the sacrament of confirmation. It is a new gift of the Holy Spirit, conferred for the

sake of an active Christian life in a closer bond of collaboration and service to the Church in order to produce, through the evangelical counsels, new fruits of holiness and apostleship in addition to the demands of the consecration received in confirmation. The sacrament of confirmation — and the character of Christian commitment and Christian apostleship that it entails — is also at the root of consecrated life.

220. In this regard it is correct to see effects of *baptism* and *confirmation* in the consecration implied by accepting the evangelical counsels and to situate religious life, which by its nature is charismatic, in the sacramental economy. Along these lines, we can also note that, for religious priests, the sacrament of *Orders* also bears fruit in the practice of the evangelical counsels, requiring a closer attachment to the Lord. The vows of chastity, poverty, and obedience aim at the concrete realization of this attachment.

The connection between the evangelical counsels and the sacraments of baptism, confirmation and Holy Orders helps to show the essential value that consecrated life represents for the growth of the Church's holiness. And for this reason I wish to close by inviting you to pray — to pray a great deal — that the Lord will increasingly bestow the gift of consecrated life on the Church that he himself willed and established as "holy."

31

"THE EVANGELICAL COUNSELS
AS A WAY OF PERFECTION"

November 9, 1994

221. The way of the evangelical counsels has often
been called a "way of perfection," and the state of
consecrated life the "state of perfection." These terms
are also found in the Council's Constitution *Lumen
gentium* (cf. n. 45), while the Decree on the renewal of
religious life is entitled *Perfectae caritatis* and has as its
theme the "pursuit of perfect charity by means of the
evangelical counsels" *(Perfectae caritatis,* n. 1).

A *way of perfection* obviously means a way of
perfection *to be acquired,* and not of a perfection *already
acquired,* as Saint Thomas Aquinas explains clearly (cf.
Summa Theol., II-II, q. 184, aa. 5, 7). Those who are
committed to the practice of the evangelical counsels do
not at all claim to possess perfection. They acknowledge
that they are sinners like all men, sinners who have been
saved. But they feel and are more expressly called to
strive for perfection, which consists essentially in charity
(cf. *ibid.,* q. 184, aa. 1, 3).

222. It cannot be forgotten that all Christians are
called to perfection. Jesus Christ himself referred
to this call: "Be perfect as your heavenly Father is
perfect" (Mt 5:48). In discussing the Church's universal
call to holiness, the Second Vatican Council says that
this holiness "is expressed in many ways by the individuals who, each in his own state of life tend to the
perfection of love, thus helping others to grow in
holiness" (*Lumen gentium,* n. 39; cf. n. 40). Nevertheless,
the universality of this call does not prevent others from

being called *in a particular way* to a life of perfection. According to Matthew's account, Jesus addressed his call to the rich young man by saying: "If you wish to be perfect..." (Mt. 19:21). This is the Gospel source of the idea of a "way of perfection": the rich young man had asked Jesus about "what is good," and in reply he received a list of the commandments; but, at the time of the call, he was invited to a perfection that goes beyond the commandments: he was called to renounce everything in order to follow Jesus. Perfection consists in the most complete gift of self to Christ. In this sense the way of the evangelical counsels is a "way of perfection" for those who are called to it.

223.   It should again be noted that the perfection Jesus offered the rich young man does not mean harm to one's person but rather its enrichment. Jesus invites the young man to renounce a plan of life in which concern about *having* is the focal point, in order for him to discover the true value of personal fulfillment in giving oneself to others and particularly in generous devotion to the Savior. Thus we can say that the real and considerable renunciations demanded by the evangelical counsels do not have a "depersonalizing" effect, but are aimed at perfecting personal life, as the result of a supernatural grace corresponding to the human being's deepest and noblest aspirations. In this regard Saint Thomas speaks of "spiritualis libertas" and "augmentum spirituale": spiritual freedom and growth (*ibid.*, II-II, q. 184, a. 4).

224.   What are the main elements of freedom and growth involved in the evangelical counsels for whoever professes them?

First of all, there is a conscious striving for the perfection of *faith*. The response to the call: "Follow me," with the renunciations it entails, requires an ardent faith in the divine person of Christ and absolute trust in his love. Both will have to grow and be strengthened along the way to avoid yielding to adversity.

Nor can a conscious striving for the perfection of *hope* be lacking. Christ's request must be viewed in the perspective of eternal life. Those who commit themselves to it are called to a firm, solid hope both at the time of their profession and throughout their life. This will allow them to witness, amid the relative, fleeting goods of this world, to the everlasting value of the goods of heaven.

225. The profession of the evangelical counsels particularly develops a conscious striving for the perfection of one's *love for God.* The Second Vatican Council speaks of the consecration produced by the evangelical counsels as the gift of self to God who is "supremely loved" (*Lumen gentium,* n. 44). It is the fulfillment of the first commandment: "You shall love the Lord your God with all your heart, and with all your soul, and with all your strength" (Dt 6:5; cf. Mk 12:30 and par.). Consecrated life genuinely grows by the continual deepening of this initial gift and by an ever stronger and more sincere love in its *Trinitarian* dimension: it is love for Christ who calls us to intimacy with him, for the Holy Spirit who seeks and helps us to become completely open to his inspirations, for the Father, the original source and ultimate goal of consecrated life. This takes place particularly in prayer, but also in every action, which receives a decidedly vertical dimension from the infused virtue of religion.

226. Obviously faith, hope and love arouse and increasingly heighten the striving for perfection of one's *love of neighbor,* as an expansion of one's love of God. The "gift of self to God who is supremely loved" implies an intense love of neighbor: love that strives to

be as perfect as possible, in imitation of the Savior's charity.

The truth of consecrated life as union with Christ in divine charity is expressed in certain basic attitudes, which should increase throughout one's life. In a general way they can be described as follows: the desire to pass on to others the love that comes from God through the Heart of Christ, and thus, the universality of a love that cannot be stopped by the barriers human selfishness creates in the name of race, nationality, cultural tradition, social or religious status, etc.; an effort to show goodwill and esteem towards all, most especially towards those who, humanly speaking, tend to be more neglected or despised; showing special solidarity to the poor and the victims of persecution and injustice; care in helping the suffering, such as the many today who are handicapped, forsaken, exiled, etc.; the witness of a meek and humble heart, which refrains from condemning, renounces all violence and revenge, and forgives joyfully; the desire to foster reconciliation everywhere and to welcome the Gospel gift of peace; generous dedication in every apostolic endeavor that seeks to spread the light of Christ and bring salvation to mankind; assiduous prayer according to the principal intentions of the Holy Father and the Church.

227.   There are many vast fields that today more than ever call for the work of "consecrated persons," as an expression of divine charity in the concrete forms of human solidarity. In many cases, perhaps, they can accomplish, humanly speaking, only little, or at least quiet, low-key things. But even small contributions are effective, if imbued with true love (the only truly great and powerful "thing"), especially if it is the same Trinitarian love poured out in the Church and the world. "Consecrated persons" are called to be these humble, faithful collaborators in the Church's progress in the world along the path of charity.

32

"CONSECRATED CHASTITY"

November 16, 1994

228. Outstanding among the evangelical counsels, according to the Second Vatican Council, is the precious gift of "perfect continence for the sake of the Kingdom of heaven": a gift of divine grace, "granted to some by the Father (cf. Mt 19:11; 1 Cor 7:7), so that in the state of virginity or celibacy they may more easily devote themselves to God alone with an undivided heart (cf. 1 Cor 7:32-34)... a sign and stimulus of charity and a singular source of fruitfulness in the world" (Constitution *Lumen gentium*, n. 42). Traditionally, "three vows" are usually spoken of — poverty, chastity and obedience — beginning with the discussion of *poverty* as detachment from external goods, ranked on a lower level with regard to the goods of body and soul (cf. Saint Thomas, *Summa Theol.*, II-II, q. 186, a. 3). The Council, instead, expressly mentions "consecrated chastity" before the other two vows (cf. *Lumen gentium*, n. 43; Decree *Perfectae caritatis*, nn. 12, 13, 14), because it considers chastity as the determining commitment of the state of consecrated life. It is also the evangelical counsel that most obviously shows the power of grace, which raises love beyond the human being's natural inclinations.

229. Its spiritual greatness stands out in the Gospel, because Jesus himself explained the value he placed on commitment to the way of celibacy. According to Matthew, Jesus praised voluntary celibacy after he asserted the indissolubility of marriage. Since Jesus forbade husbands to divorce their wives, the disciples reacted: "If such is the case of a man with his wife, it is

not expedient to marry." And Jesus answered by giving the "it is not expedient to marry" a deeper meaning: "Not all men can receive this precept, but only those to whom it is given. For there are eunuchs who have been so from birth, and there are eunuchs who have been made eunuchs by men, and there are eunuchs who have made themselves eunuchs for the sake of the Kingdom of heaven. He who is able to receive this, let him receive it" (Mt 19:10-12).

230.   In stating this possibility of understanding a new way, which was that practiced by him and the disciples, and which perhaps led those around them to wonder or even to criticize, Jesus used an image that alluded to a well-known fact, the condition of "eunuchs." They could be such because of a congenital imperfection or because of human intervention: but he immediately added that there was a new category — his! — "eunuchs for the sake of the Kingdom of heaven." It was an obvious reference to the choice he made and recommended to his closest followers. According to the Mosaic law, eunuchs were excluded from worship (Dt 23:2) and the priesthood (Lv 21:20). An oracle in the Book of Isaiah had foretold the end of this exclusion (Is 56:3-5). Jesus opens an even more innovative horizon: the voluntary choice "for the sake of the Kingdom of heaven" of this situation considered unworthy of man. Obviously, Jesus' words did not mean an actual physical mutilation, which the Church has never permitted, but the free renunciation of sexual relations. As I wrote in the Apostolic Exhortation *Redemptionis donum*, this means a "renunciation therefore — the reflection of the mystery of Calvary — in order 'to be' more fully in the crucified and risen Christ; renunciation in order to recognize fully in him the mystery of one's own human nature, and to confirm this on the path of that wonderful process of which the same Apostle writes in another

place: 'Though our outer nature is wasting away, our inner nature is being renewed every day' (2 Cor 4:16)" (n. 10).

231. Jesus is aware of the values renounced by those who live in perpetual celibacy: he himself affirmed them shortly before when he spoke of marriage as a union of which God is the author and which therefore cannot be broken. Being committed to celibacy does indeed mean renouncing the goods inherent in married life and the family, but never ceasing to appreciate them for their real value. The renunciation is made in view of a greater good, of higher values, summed up in the beautiful Gospel expression of the "Kingdom of heaven." The complete gift of self to this Kingdom justifies and sanctifies celibacy.

232. Jesus calls attention to the gift of divine light needed to "understand" the way of voluntary celibacy. Not everyone can understand it, in the sense that not everyone is "able" to grasp its meaning, to accept it, to practice it. This gift of light and decision is only granted to some. It is a privilege granted them for the sake of a greater love. We should not be surprised then if many, who do not understand the value of consecrated celibacy, are not attracted to it, and often are not even able to appreciate it. This means that there is a variety of ways, charisms and roles, as Saint Paul recognized. He spontaneously wished to share his ideal of virginal life with everyone. He wrote: "I wish that all were as I myself am. But each," he adds, "has his own special gift from God, one of one kind and one of another" (1 Cor 7:7). Moreover, as Saint Thomas observed, "the Church derives a certain beauty from the variety of states" (*Summa Theol.*, II-II, q. 184, a. 4).

233.   For his part, the individual is required to make a
        deliberate act of will, conscious of the duty and
the privilege of consecrated celibacy. This does not
mean simply abstaining from marriage, nor an unmoti-
vated and almost passive observance of the norms
imposed by chastity. The act of renunciation has a
positive aspect in the total dedication to the Kingdom,
which implies absolute devotion to God "who is supremely loved" and to the service of his Kingdom.
Therefore, the choice must be well-thought out and
stem from a firm, conscious decision that has matured
deep within the individual.

Saint Paul states the demands and advantages of
this dedication to the Kingdom: "The unmarried man is
anxious about the affairs of the Lord, how to please the
Lord; but the married man is anxious about worldly
affairs, how to please his wife, and his interests are
divided. And the unmarried woman or girl is anxious
about the affairs of the Lord, how to be holy in body and
spirit; but the married woman is anxious about worldly
affairs, how to please her husband" (1 Cor 7: 32-34). The
Apostle does not mean to condemn the married state
(cf. 1 Tm 4:1-3), nor "to lay any restraint" on anyone, as
he said (1 Cor 7:35); but with the realism of experience
enlightened by the Holy Spirit, he speaks and counsels
— as he wrote — "for your own benefit ... to promote
good order and to secure your undivided devotion to
the Lord" (*ibid.*). This is the purpose of the evangelical
counsels. And the Second Vatican Council, faithful to
the tradition of the counsels, states that chastity is "a
most effective means of dedicating themselves wholeheartedly to the divine service and the works of the
apostolate" (*Perfectae caritatis,* n. 12).

234.   "Consecrated celibacy" has been criticized over
        and over again in history, and many times the
Church has had to call attention to the excellence of the

religious state in this regard: one need only recall the Declaration of the Council of Trent (cf. DS 1810), cited by Pius XII in the Encyclical *Sacra virginitas* because of its magisterial value (cf. AAS 46 [1954], 174). This does not mean casting a shadow on the married state. Instead we must keep in mind what the *Catechism of the Catholic Church* states: "Both the sacrament of Matrimony and virginity for the Kingdom of God come from the Lord himself. It is he who gives them meaning and grants them the grace which is indispensable for living them out in conformity with his will. Esteem of virginity for the sake of the Kingdom and the Christian understanding of marriage are inseparable, and they reinforce each other" (n. 1620; cf. Apost. Exhortation *Redemptionis donum*, n. 11).

235.   The Second Vatican Council warns that accepting and observing the evangelical counsel of consecrated virginity and celibacy requires "sufficient psychological and emotional maturity" (*Perfectae caritatis*, n. 12). This maturity is indispensable.

Hence, the conditions for faithfully following Christ on this point are: trust in God's love and prayer to him stirred by the awareness of human weakness; prudent and humble behavior; and above all, a life of intense union with Christ.

This last point, which is the key to all consecrated life, contains the secret of fidelity to Christ as the one Bridegroom of the soul, the only reason to live.

33

"CONSECRATED CHASTITY AND CHRIST'S NUPTIAL UNION WITH THE CHURCH"

November 23, 1994

236. According to the Council's Decree *Perfectae caritatis*, religious "give witness to all Christ's faithful of that *wondrous marriage* made by God, which will be fully manifested in the future age, and in which the Church has Christ for her only spouse" (n. 12). It is in this marriage that the basic value of virginity or celibacy in relation to God is discovered. It is for this reason that one speaks of *"consecrated chastity."*

The truth of this marriage is revealed by many statements in the New Testament. We remember that the Baptist called Jesus the bridegroom who has the bride, i.e., the people who rushed to his baptism; while he, John, sees himself as the "groom's best man who waits there listening for him and is overjoyed to hear his voice" (Jn 3:29). This marriage imagery was already used in the Old Testament to indicate the close relationship between God and Israel: the prophets especially, after Hosea (1:2ff.), used it to exalt that relationship and to call the people back to it if they had betrayed it (cf. Is 1:21; Jer 2:2; 3:1; 3:6-12; Ez 16; 23). In the second part of the Book of Isaiah, the restoration of Israel is described as the reconciliation of an unfaithful wife with her husband (cf. Is 50:1; 54:5-8; 62:4-5). The presence of this imagery in the religious faith of Israel also appears in the Song of Songs and in Psalm 45, wedding songs prefiguring the marriage with the Messiah King, as they were interpreted by Jewish and Christian tradition.

237.   Within the context of his people's tradition, Jesus made use of the imagery to say that he himself is the Bridegroom foretold and awaited: the Messiah Bridegroom (cf. Mt 9:15; 25:1). He insists on this analogy and terminology to explain what the "Kingdom" is that he has come to bring. "The reign of God may be likened to a king who gave a wedding banquet for his son" (Mt 22:2). He compares his disciples to the bridegroom's friends, who rejoice at his presence and will fast when the bridegroom is taken away from them (cf. Mk 2:19-20). There is also the well-known parable of the ten virgins waiting for the bridegroom to arrive for the wedding feast (cf. Mt 25:1-13), as well as that of the servants who must be watching to welcome their master when he returns from a wedding (cf. Lk 12:35-38). In this regard it could be said that the first miracle Jesus performed at Cana, precisely at a wedding banquet, is significant (cf. Jn 2:1-11).

238.   By calling himself the Bridegroom, Jesus expressed the meaning of his entrance into history: he came to bring about God's marriage with humanity, in accordance with what the prophets foretold, in order to establish Yahweh's New Covenant with his people, and to fill human hearts with the new gift of divine love and enable them to taste its joy. As the Bridegroom, he invites everyone to respond to this gift of love: all are called to answer love with love. He asks some to give a fuller, stronger and more radical response: that of virginity or celibacy "for the Kingdom of heaven."

We also know that Saint Paul accepted and developed the imagery of Christ the Bridegroom suggested by the Old Testament and taken up by Jesus in his preaching and in teaching the disciples whom he would establish as the first community. The Apostle urges those who are married to consider the example of the messianic marriage: "Husbands, love your wives as

Christ loved the Church" (Eph 5:25). But in addition to this special application, he looks on the Christian life in the perspective of a spousal union with Christ: "I have given you in marriage to one husband, presenting you as a chaste virgin to Christ" (2 Cor 11:2).

239.   Paul wishes to make this presentation to Christ the Bridegroom for all Christians. However, there is no doubt that the Pauline imagery of the chaste virgin finds its full realization and its greatest meaning in consecrated chastity. The most splendid model of this fulfillment is the Virgin Mary, who accepted in her being the best of her people's marital tradition, not limiting herself to the awareness of her special belonging to God on the socio-religious level, but applying the idea of Israel as bride to the complete giving of her soul and body "for the Kingdom of heaven," in her sublime form of consciously chosen chastity. Hence the Council could state that in the Church the consecrated life is lived in deep harmony with the Blessed Virgin Mary (cf. *Lumen gentium*, n. 46), who is presented by the Church as "the one most fully consecrated" (cf. *Redemptionis donum*, n. 17).

240.   In the Christian world a new light was shed by Christ's word and Mary's example of oblation, a light soon to be known by the first communities. The reference to the nuptial union of Christ and the Church gives marriage itself its highest dignity: in particular, the sacrament of matrimony introduces the spouses into the mystery of Christ's union with the Church. However, the profession of virginity or celibacy enables consecrated persons to share more directly in the mystery of this marriage. While conjugal love goes to Christ the Bridegroom through a human union, virginal love goes directly to the person of Christ through an immediate union with him, without intermediaries: a truly

complete and decisive spiritual espousal. Thus in the person of those who profess and live consecrated chastity, the Church expresses her union as Bride with Christ the Bridegroom to the greatest extent. For this reason it must be said that the virginal life is found at the heart of the Church.

241.   In line with the evangelical and Christian concept, it must also be said that this immediate union with the Bridegroom is an anticipation of the life of heaven, which will be characterized by a vision or possession of God without intermediaries. As the Second Vatican Council said, consecrated chastity "gives witness to all Christ's faithful of that wondrous marriage made by God, which will be fully manifested in the future age" (*Perfectae caritatis,* n. 12). In the Church the state of virginity or celibacy thus has an eschatological meaning, as a particularly expressive foretaste of the possession of Christ as the one Bridegroom, as will occur in the fullness of the life to come. This is the meaning of what Jesus said about the state of life which will belong to the elect after the resurrection of the body: they "neither marry nor are given in marriage. They become like angels who are no longer liable to death. Sons of the resurrection (= raised up), they are sons of God" (Lk 20:35-36). The state of consecrated chastity, despite the obscurities and difficulties of earthly life, foreshadows the union with God, in Christ, which the elect will have in heavenly happiness, when the spiritualization of the risen man will be complete.

242.   The profound happiness of consecrated life is understood from a consideration of this goal of heavenly union with Christ the Bridegroom. Saint Paul refers to this happiness when he says that the unmarried man is busy with the Lord's affairs and is not divided between the world and the Lord (cf. 1 Cor 7: 32-35). But

this is a happiness from which sacrifice is neither excluded nor dispensed with, since consecrated celibacy involves renunciations by which one is called to be more closely conformed to Christ crucified. Saint Paul expressly states that in his Bridegroom's love, Jesus Christ offered his sacrifice for the holiness of the Church (cf. Eph 5:25). In the light of the Cross, we understand that every union with Christ the Bridegroom is a loving commitment to the One who was crucified, since those who profess consecrated chastity know they are destined to a deeper sharing in Christ's sacrifice for the redemption of the world (cf. *Redemptionis donum,* nn. 8, 11).

243. The permanent nature of the nuptial union of Christ and the Church is expressed in the definitive value of the profession of consecrated chastity in religious life. "And this consecration will be the more perfect inasmuch as by firmer and more stable bonds Christ is more clearly seen to be united to his Bride the Church by an indissoluble bond" (*Lumen gentium,* n. 44). The indissolubility of the Church's covenant with Christ the Bridegroom, shared in the pledge of self-giving to Christ in the virginal life, is the basis for the permanent validity of perpetual profession. It could be said that it is an absolute gift to him who is the Absolute. Jesus himself makes this clear when he says: "Whoever puts his hand to the plough but keeps looking back is unfit for the reign of God" (Lk 9:62). Permanence, fidelity in the commitment to religious life, is clarified in the light of this Gospel saying.

244. With their witness of fidelity to Christ, consecrated persons support the fidelity of couples themselves in their marriage. The task of giving this support underlies Jesus' statement about those who become eunuchs for the sake of the Kingdom of heaven

(cf. Mt 19:10-12): by this statement the Master wishes to show that the indissolubility of marriage — which he had just enunciated — is not impossible to observe, as the disciples were implying, because there are people who, with the help of grace, live outside marriage in perfect continence.

Hence we see that, far from being opposed to one another, consecrated celibacy and marriage are joined in the divine plan. Together they are meant to make the union of Christ and the Church more visible.

34

"EVANGELICAL POVERTY, ESSENTIAL CONDITION FOR THE CONSECRATED LIFE"

November 30, 1994

245.   In the contemporary world, with its blatant contrast between the forms of greed — both ancient and new — and the situations of unheard-of misery in which enormously broad strata of society live, the *value of poverty* freely chosen and consistently practiced is seen ever more clearly at the sociological level. From the Christian point of view, poverty has always been experienced as a state of life that makes it easier to follow Christ in contemplation, prayer and evangelization. It is important for the Church that many Christians have a deeper awareness of Christ's love for the poor and of the urgent need to come to their aid. But it is equally true that conditions in contemporary society point ever more harshly to the distance between the Gospel of the poor and a world often absorbed in pursuing interests connected with the craving of wealth, which has become an idol holding sway over the whole of life. This is why the Church is ever more intensely aware of the Spirit's prompting to be poor among the poor, to remind everyone of the need to conform to the ideal of poverty preached and practiced by Christ and to imitate his sincere, active love for the poor.

246.   In particular, there is in the Church a revitalized and consolidated awareness of the frontline position occupied in this area of Gospel values by religious and all those who seek to follow Christ in consecrated life, called as they are to reflect in their own person and

to witness before the world to the Master's poverty and his love for the poor. He himself linked the counsel of poverty both to the need for being personally stripped of the burden of earthly belongings so as to possess the heavenly good and to charity towards the poor: "Go and sell what you have and give to the poor; you will then have treasure in heaven. After that, come and follow me" (Mk 10:21).

247.   In asking for this renunciation, Jesus set for the rich young man a prior condition for "following" him, which consisted in the most complete sharing possible in the self-emptying of the Incarnation. Paul reminded the Christians of Corinth of this to encourage them to be generous with the poor, imitating the example of Christ, who "he made himself poor though he was rich, so that you might become rich by his poverty" (2 Cor 8:9). Saint Thomas comments; Jesus "endured material poverty to give us spiritual riches" (*Summa Theol.*, III, q. 40, a. 3). Everyone who accepts his invitation and voluntarily follows the way of poverty he inaugurated is led to enrich the human race spiritually. Far from simply adding their poverty to that of the other poor who fill the world, they are called to bring them true wealth, which is spiritual in nature. As I wrote in the Apostolic Exhortation *Redemptionis donum,* Christ "is the teacher and spokesman of poverty who makes us rich" (n. 12).

248.   If we look at this Teacher, we learn from him the true meaning of Gospel poverty and the greatness of the call to follow him on the path of this poverty. First of all, we see that Jesus really lived like the poor. According to Saint Paul, he, the Son of God, embraced the human condition as one of poverty, and in this human condition he lived a life of poverty. His birth was that of a poor person, as shown by the stable in which he

was born and the manger in which his Mother placed him. For thirty years he lived in a family in which Joseph earned his daily bread by working as a carpenter, work he himself later shared (cf. Mt 13:55; Mk 6:3). In his public life he could say of himself: "The Son of Man has nowhere to lay his head" (Lk 9:58), as if to show his total dedication to his messianic mission in conditions of poverty. He died as a slave and poor man, literally stripped of everything, on the Cross. He chose to be poor to the very end.

249. Jesus proclaimed the blessedness of the poor: "Blest are you poor; the reign of God is yours" (Lk 6:20). In this regard we should remember that the Old Testament already spoke of the "Lord's poor" (cf. Ps 74:19; 149:4ff.), the object of God's goodwill (Is 49:13; 66:2). This does not mean simply the destitute, but rather the lowly who sought God and trustfully put themselves under his protection. This attitude of humility and trust clarifies the expression used in the Evangelist Matthew's version of the Beatitudes: "How blest are the poor in spirit" (Mt 5:3). The "poor in spirit" are all those who do not put their trust in money or material possessions, and are open instead to the Kingdom of God. However, it is precisely this value of poverty that Jesus praises and recommends as a life choice, which can include a voluntary renunciation of belongings, and precisely so on behalf of the poor. It is the *privilege of some* who are chosen and called to this way by him.

250. Jesus however affirms *for everyone the need* to make a basic decision regarding earthly goods: to be freed of their tyranny. No one, he says, can serve two masters. One either serves God or serves Mammon (cf. Lk 16:13; Mt 6:24). The idolatry of Mammon, or money, is incompatible with serving God. Jesus notes that the rich are more easily attached to money (called mamona

in Aramaic, meaning "riches"), and have difficulty in turning to God: "How hard it will be for the rich to enter the Kingdom of God! Indeed, it is easier for a camel to go through a needle's eye than for a rich man to enter the Kingdom of heaven" (Lk 18:24-25; par.).

251.   Jesus warns against the twofold danger of earthly possessions: that with wealth one's heart is closed to God and is also closed to one's neighbor, as we see in the parable of the rich man and Lazarus (cf. Lk 16:19-31). Nevertheless, Jesus does not condemn the possession of earthly goods absolutely: he is instead anxious to remind those who own them of the twofold commandment of love of God and love of neighbor. But he asks much more of anyone who can and wishes to understand so.

The Gospel is clear on this point: Jesus asks those he called and invited to follow him to share his own poverty by renouncing their possessions, however great or few they may be. We already quoted his invitation to the rich young man: "Sell what you have and give to the poor" (Mk 10:21). It was a fundamental requirement, repeated many times, which meant giving up home and property (cf. Mk 10:29; par.), or boat (cf. Mt 4:22), or even everything: "None of you can be my disciple if he does not renounce all his possessions" (Lk 14:33). To his "disciples," that is to those called to follow him by totally giving of themselves, Jesus said: "Sell what you have and give alms" (Lk 12:33).

252.   This poverty is asked of those who are willing to follow Christ in consecrated life. Their poverty is expressed concretely in a juridical way, as the Council recalls. It can take various forms: the radical renunciation of owning property, as in the ancient "mendicant Orders," and as practiced today by the members of other religious Congregations (cf. Decree *Perfectae*

216

caritatis, n. 13), and other possible forms which the Council encourages to be sought (cf. *ibid.*). What matters is that poverty be really lived as a sharing in Christ's poverty: "With regard to religious poverty it is by no means enough to be subject to superiors in the use of property. Religious should be poor in fact and in spirit, having their treasures in heaven (cf. Mt 6:20)" (*Perfectae caritatis*, n. 13).

253. Institutes themselves are called to a *collective* witness to poverty. Giving new authority to the voice of so many teachers of spirituality and religious life, the Council particularly stressed that Institutes "should avoid any semblance of luxury, excessive wealth and accumulation of property" (*Perfectae caritatis*, n. 13). And again, their poverty should be animated by a spirit of sharing between various provinces and houses, and of generosity "for the needs of the Church and for the support of the poor" (*ibid.*).

254. Another point, which is emerging again and again in the recent development of the forms of poverty, is seen in the Council's recommendation concerning "the common law of labor" (*Perfectae caritatis*, n. 13). In the past, there was the choice and practice of begging, a sign of poverty, humility and beneficial charity towards the needy. Today it is rather by their labor that religious "are provided with whatever they need for their sustenance or their work." It is a law of life and a practice of poverty. Embracing it freely and joyfully means accepting the counsel and believing in the Gospel blessedness of poverty. It is the greatest service that in this respect religious can give to the Gospel: witnessing to and practicing the spirit of trusting abandonment into the Father's hands as true followers of Christ, who lived and taught that spirit and left it as an inheritance to his Church.

35

"EVANGELICAL OBEDIENCE IN THE CONSECRATED LIFE"

December 7, 1994

255.   When Jesus called disciples to follow him, he taught them the need for *an obedience devoted to his person*. This was not only a question of the common observance of the divine law and the dictates of a true and upright human conscience, but of a much greater commitment. Following Christ meant being willing to do all that he personally commanded and putting oneself under his direction in serving the Gospel for the coming of God's Kingdom (cf. Lk 9:60, 62).

Therefore, in addition to the commitment to celibacy and poverty, with his "Follow me," Jesus also asked for one of obedience, which extended to the disciples his own obedience to the Father in the condition of the Incarnate Word who became the "Servant of Yahweh" (cf. Is 42:1; 52:13-53; 12; Phil 2:7). Like poverty and chastity, obedience thus marked the fulfillment of Jesus' mission and indeed was its basic principle, expressed in the very intense feeling that led him to say: "My food is to do the will of him who sent me, and to accomplish his work" (Jn 4:34; cf. *Redemptions donum,* n. 13). We know from the Gospel that in virtue of this attitude, Jesus went so far as the sacrifice of the Cross with total self-dedication, when — as Saint Paul wrote — he who was divine in nature "humbled himself and became obedient unto death, even death on a cross" (Phil 2:8). The *Letter to the Hebrews* stresses that Jesus Christ "although he was Son, learned obedience through what he suffered" (Heb 5:8).

256.   Jesus himself revealed that his heart's desire was to sacrifice himself totally, as it were through a mysterious *pondus Crucis* (weight of the Cross), a sort of law of gravity of immolated life, which would find its greatest expression in the prayer of Gethsemane; "Abba, Father, all things are possible to you; remove this cup from me; yet not what I will, but what you will" (Mk 14:36).

Heirs of the disciples directly called by Jesus to follow him in his messianic mission, religious — the Council says — "by their profession of obedience, offer the full dedication of their own wills as a sacrifice of themselves to God, and by this means they are united more permanently and securely with God's saving will" (*Perfectae caritatis*, n. 14). Their response to God's saving will justifies the renunciation of their own freedom. As openness to God's saving plan against the limitless horizon in which the Father embraces all creation, evangelical obedience goes far beyond the disciple's personal destiny: it is a sharing in the work of universal Redemption.

257.   This salvific value was underscored by Saint Paul in regard to Christ's obedience. If sin came into the world through an act of disobedience, universal salvation was obtained by the Redeemer's obedience: "For as by one man's disobedience many were made sinners, so by one man's obedience many will be made righteous" (Rom 5:19). In the patristic literature of the early centuries the parallel Saint Paul made between Adam and Christ was taken up and developed, as was the reference to Mary in relation to Eve, from the aspect of obedience. Saint Irenaeus wrote: "The knot of Eve's disobedience was loosed by Mary's obedience" (*Adversus haereses,* III, 22, 4). "As the former was seduced into disobeying God, so the latter was convinced to obey God" (*ibid.*). For this reason Mary became the coopera-

tor of salvation: *Causa salutis (ibid.)*. By their obedience religious are also deeply involved in the work of salvation.

258. Saint Thomas sees in religious obedience the most perfect form of imitating Christ, who Saint Paul says "became obedient unto death, even death on a cross" (Phil 2:8). Obedience thus holds the chief place in the holocaust of religious profession (cf. *Summa Theol.*, II-II, q. 186, aa. 5, 7, 8).

Following this strong, beautiful Christian tradition, the Council states: "After the example of Jesus Christ ... religious moved by the Holy Spirit subject themselves in faith to those who hold God's place, their superiors. Through them they are led to serve all their brothers in Christ, just as Christ ministered to his brothers in submission to the Father and laid down his life for the redemption of many" (*Perfectae caritatis,* n. 14). Obedience to the Father was lived by Jesus without excluding human intermediaries. As a child Jesus obeyed Joseph and Mary: Saint Luke says that he "was obedient to them" (Lk 2:51).

259. Thus Jesus is the model for those who obey human authority by perceiving in this authority a sign of God's will. By the evangelical counsel of obedience religious are called to obey their superiors as God's representatives. For this reason, in explaining a text (ch. 68 of Saint Benedict's *Rule)*, Saint Thomas asserts that religious must abide by the judgment of the superior (cf. *Summa Theol.*, I-II, q. 13, a. 5, ad 3).

It is easy to understand that the difficulty of obedience often lies in perceiving this divine representation in a human creature. But if the mystery of the Cross appears here, it should be kept in view. It should always be remembered that religious obedience is not simply a human submission to a human authority.

Whoever obeys, submits himself to God, to the divine will expressed in the will of the superiors. It is a matter of faith. Religious must believe in God who communicates his will to them through their superiors. Even when the superiors' faults are apparent, their will, if not contrary to the law of God or to the Rule, expresses the divine will. Even when from the standpoint of human judgment the decision does not seem wise, a faith judgment accepts the mystery of God's will: *mysterium Crucis*.

260. Moreover, human mediation, though imperfect, bears a stamp of authenticity: that of the Church, which by her authority approves religious Institutes and their laws as sure ways of Christian perfection. In addition to this reason of an ecclesial nature there is another stemming from the purpose of religious Institutes: "to contribute towards the building up of the Body of Christ according to God's plan" (*Perfectae caritatis*, n. 14). For the religious who regards and practices obedience in this way, it becomes the secret of true happiness given by the Christian certitude of having followed God's will instead of his own, with an intense love for Christ and the Church.

In addition, the Council urges superiors first to be docile to God's will, to be aware of their responsibility, to foster a spirit of service, to show charity to their brethren, to respect their subjects as human persons, to create an atmosphere of cooperation, to listen to their brethren willingly, while retaining their authority to make decisions (cf. *Perfectae caritatis*, n. 14).

261. Love for the Church was at the origin of the Rules and Constitutions of religious families, which sometimes expressly declared their pledge of submission to Church authority. This explains the example of Saint Ignatius of Loyola, who, in order better to serve

Christ and the Church, gave the Society of Jesus the famous "fourth vow" of "special obedience to the Pope concerning the missions." This vow states explicitly a norm that was and is implicit in any religious profession. Other Institutes have also made this norm explicit in one way or another.

262. Today the Code of Canon Law emphasizes it, in accord with the best tradition of Gospel teaching and spirituality: "Institutes of consecrated life, inasmuch as they are dedicated in a special way to the service of God and of the entire Church, are subject to the supreme authority of this same Church in a particular manner" (can. 590, § 1). "Individual members (of Institutes) are also bound to obey the Supreme Pontiff as their highest superior by reason of the sacred bond of obedience" (*ibid.*, § 2). These are norms of life, which, when embraced and followed in faith, lead religious far beyond a juridical idea of structural organization in the Christian community: they feel the need to be as involved as possible in the Church's spiritual propensities and apostolic endeavors, in the various moments of her life, by their actions or at least by their prayer, and always with their filial affection.

36

"COMMON LIFE IN THE LIGHT
OF THE GOSPEL"

December 14, 1994

263. Regarding the essential aspects of consecrated life, the Second Vatican Council, in the Decree *Perfectae caritatis*, after discussing the evangelical counsels of chastity, poverty and obedience, speaks of *life in common* with reference to the example of the first Christian communities and in the light of the Gospel.

The Council's teaching on this point is very important, even though it is true that a life in common, strictly understood, does not exist or is greatly reduced in some forms of consecrated life, such as the eremitic, while it is not necessarily required in secular Institutes. It exists however in the great majority of Institutes of consecrated life and has always been considered by founders and by the Church as a basic observance for the good progress of religious life and the effective organization of the apostolate. As a confirmation of this, the Congregation for Institutes of Consecrated Life and Societies of Apostolic Life recently published (February 2, 1994) a special document on "Fraternal Life in Community."

264. If we look at the Gospel, it could be said that life in common is a response to Jesus' *teaching* on the connection between the two precepts of love of God and love of neighbor. In a state of life in which God is supremely loved, one cannot but strive to love one's neighbor with particular generosity, beginning with those who are closest because they belong to the same

community. This is the state of life of "consecrated" persons.

Moreover, it is clear from the Gospel that Jesus' *calls* were addressed, indeed, to individuals but usually in order to invite them to join, to form a group: this was the case with the group of disciples and with that of the women.

265. The Gospel text documents the importance of fraternal charity as the soul of the community, and thus as an essential value of the common life. There is a reference to the disputes which took place on several occasions between the Apostles themselves, who in following Jesus did not cease to be men, children of their time and their people: they were anxious to establish ranks of greatness and authority. Jesus' response was a lesson in humility and willingness to serve (cf. Mt 18:3-4; 20:26-28; par.). Then he gave them "his" commandment of mutual love (cf. Jn 13:34; 15:12, 17) according to his example. In the history of the Church, particularly in that of religious Institutes, the question of the relationship between individuals and groups has often been raised, and it has no other valid answer than that of Christian humility and fraternal love, which unites in the name and power of Christ's love, as the ancient song of the "agapes" says over and over; *Congregavit nos in unum Christi amor,* the love of Christ has gathered us together.

266. Certainly, the practice of fraternal love in the common life requires considerable effort and sacrifice, and demands generosity no less than the practice of the evangelical counsels. Hence, joining a religious Institute or community implies a serious commitment to living fraternal love in all its aspects.

267. An example of this is found in the first Christian community. They came together immediately after the Ascension to pray in unity of heart (cf. Acts 1:14) and to persevere in fraternal "communion" (Acts 2:42), going so far as to share their possessions: "they shared all things in common" (Acts 2:44). The unity desired by Christ found, at the time of the Church's beginning, a fulfillment worthy of being recorded: "The community of believers were of one heart and one mind" (Acts 4:32).

The Church has always retained a deep memory of—perhaps even a nostalgia for—that early community and basically, religious communities have always sought to reproduce that ideal of communion in charity as a practical rule of life in common. Their members, gathered by the love of Christ, live together because they intend to abide in this love. Thus they can witness to the Church's true countenance, which reflects her soul: charity.

"One heart and one mind" does not mean a rigid, featureless uniformity, but a deep communion in mutual understanding and reciprocal respect.

268. It cannot only be a matter, however, of a union of like-mindedness and human affection. The Council, echoing the Acts of the Apostles, speaks of a "sharing of the same spirit" (*Perfectae caritatis,* n. 15). It is a question of a unity that has its deepest root in the Holy Spirit, who pours out his love into hearts (cf. Rom 5:5) and spurs different people to help one another on the path of perfection by creating and maintaining an atmosphere of good understanding and cooperation among themselves. As the guarantee of unity in the whole Church, the Holy Spirit establishes it and causes it to abide in an even more intense way in communities of consecrated life.

269. What are the ways of this charity infused by the Holy Spirit? The Council calls particular attention to mutual esteem (cf. *Perfectae caritatis,* n. 15). It applies to religious two of Saint Paul's exhortations to Christians: "Love one another with mutual affection; anticipate each other in showing respect" (Rom 12:10), and "Help carry one another's burdens" (Gal 6:2).

Mutual esteem is an expression of mutual love, which is opposed to the widespread tendency to judge one's neighbor harshly and criticize him. Paul's exhortation urges us to discover other people's qualities and, as far as the poor human eye can tell, the marvelous work of grace and — ultimately — of the Holy Spirit. This esteem means accepting the other with his characteristics and his way of thinking and acting; thus, despite many obstacles, harmony between what are often very different dispositions can be achieved.

270. "Help carry one another's burdens" means sympathetically bearing with the true or apparent defects of others, however irksome, and willingly accepting all the sacrifices required by living together with those whose mentality and temperament are not in full accord with one's own way of seeing and judging.

271. In this regard, the Council (*Perfectae caritatis,* n. 15) recalls that charity is the fulfillment of the law (cf. Rom 13:10), the bond of perfection (cf. Col 3:14), the sign of having passed from death to life (cf. 1 Jn 3:14), the manifestation of Christ's coming (cf. Jn 14:21, 23) and the source of great apostolic power. We can apply to the common life the excellence of charity described by Saint Paul in the *First Letter to the Corinthians* (13:1-13) and attribute to it what the Apostle calls the fruits of the Spirit: "love, joy, peace, patient endurance, kindness, generosity, mildness and chastity" (Gal 5:22),

fruits, — the Council says — of "the love of God which is poured into their hearts" (*Perfectae caritatis*, n. 15).

Jesus said: "Where two or three are gathered in my name, there am I in their midst" (Mt 18:20). See: Christ is present wherever there is unity in charity, and Christ's presence is the source of deep joy, which is renewed each day until the definitive meeting with him.